On The Hunt

A Talent Acquisition Expert's Life

by
Eileen Evans

This book was based on information received from Ellie Hipple, who is the talent acquisition expert referenced in the title.

Over her career, Ellie has worked at many different organizations in permanent and contract roles, which were each in different industries. Through these experiences, she mastered effectively sourcing and recruiting for a variety of industry-specialized roles internationally, as well as business support roles that are common across industries.

Ellie's experience working for five large corporations in contract capacities taught her how to quickly master hiring SOPs and processes. Through this, she became an expert full-cyle recruiter and sourcer with a broad understanding of a variety of recruitment processes, procedures, and organizational best practices.

Ellie is excited to share her talent acquisition expertise through this book. She can be reach via LinkedIn at https://Linkedin.com/in/elliehipple.

Table of Contents

Introduction

Welcome to the world of talent acquisition, an arduous yet rewarding journey that takes us deep into the human organizational structures. It's a world where strategic expertise meets innovative methodologies, leading to the creation and enhancement of truly dynamic teams. So, why should you be interested in learning about talent acquisition? Quite simply, in the ever-changing landscape of the business world, talent acquisition continues to be a critical component to organizational success. Businesses can live or die based on their ability to find, attract, and retain top-notch talent, and that's where talent acquisition professionals come in. The work that we'll be exploring ranges from a detailed understanding of roles and components in talent acquisition, through the strategic workflow of the process, and even to building a successful talent acquisition function. But it's worth noting, the success of our journey wouldn't solely rely on facts and figures; it's also about creating a human connection. So let's delve into the wonderful complexities of talent acquisition, shall we?

Understanding Talent Acquisition

Talent acquisition is an integral part of any organization's success. It's more than hiring individuals who meet the listed job qualifications. It's about understanding the organization's direction, needs, culture, and strategically identifying individuals who would push the company forward. Yet, it's often misunderstood and underappreciated, with recruiters rushing to fill vacancies without considering the bigger picture.

Talent acquisition is a proactive, strategic process, not a reactive one. It's about finding the right fit for the organization - individuals who not only do the job but also improve the organization, add value, integrate into the culture, and contribute to a positive work environment. The goal isn't just to fill a job slot. It's to bring onboard someone who can enhance the company's direction and mission.

We can't undervalue the impact of hiring on an organization's trajectory. One brilliant hire can propel the company into a new sphere of success, while a poor one can set the business back significantly. The stakes in talent acquisition are high, and the strategic implications are real. This is why it's all the more essential to grasp its intricacies.

Furthermore, talent acquisition differs from typical recruitment. The latter is a linear, short-term process aimed at filling vacant spots. The former, however, is a long-term, all-encompassing strategy designed to attract and retain people who will make a significant impact in the organization. While recruitment focuses on speed and efficiency, talent acquisition stresses quality and fit.

The scope of talent acquisition is vast. It includes sourcing, employer branding, candidate engagement, retention strategies, and much more. It's not just about finding people who can do the job. It's about finding individuals who can do the job, will thrive in the organization's culture, and are likely to stick around for a long time.

The stakes are particularly high with hard-to-fill roles or high-profile roles. These often require a deep understanding of the field, a large network of contacts, and a keen eye for quality. It takes a combination of intuition, experience, and solid data analysis to successfully fill such positions through strategic talent acquisition.

Recruiting top-notch talent is also increasingly becoming more about selling the job and the company, rather than about simply selecting the best from a lineup of candidates. In a competitive job market, recruiters must think like marketers to make their companies stand out from competitors and attract the best talent.

Another factor to consider in the talent acquisition process is the growing impact of technology. Imagine the electronic resources at our disposal! Database management systems, Applicant Tracking Systems (ATS), digital interviews, social media platforms, online networking sites - these have all transformed the talent acquisition process, making it more intensive and dynamic.

Talent acquisition is a team sport. It involves multiple departments and stakeholders, not just human resources. Among others, it includes hiring managers, team leaders, interviewers, decision-makers, even the potential new hires themselves. Everyone plays their part in creating a successful hiring process.

Culture fit is pivotal in the talent acquisition process, and it goes both ways. An employee who doesn't fit the company culture - however skilled or talented - that person won't be effective or happy. By the same token, an organization must be a cultural fit for the individual so that the employee can bring their whole self to work, thrive, and stay for the long haul.

A crucial part of talent acquisition is looking beyond the now, strategically planning for the organization's future requirements. It involves anticipating the skills and competencies the organization will need down the line, creating a robust pipeline of potential candidates, and building relationships with them—long before job openings even exist.

In essence, talent acquisition is a significant business strategy aimed at securing the organization's future, ensuring its sustainability and success. It touches on various aspects, including branding, diversity and inclusion, compensation, benefits, career development, training, succession planning, and more.

Understandably, talent acquisition can be a complicated, nuanced process. However, its intricacies and complexities are what make it an exciting field. It involves people, strategies, procedures, and evolving technologies.

To sum up, talent acquisition is a very dynamic field, and understanding it is central to any effective hiring strategy. Remember, it's not about filling a position; it's about securing a future. The future of your organization - It doesn't get more exciting than that.

So now let's dive deeper and take a look at the various roles involved in the talent acquisition process. From sourcing to employer branding, candidate engagement, and more - It's all part of understanding this vital field.

Various Roles in Talent Acquisition

Within the spectrum of talent acquisition, there's a wide variety of roles that contribute to the critical task of finding, attracting, and retaining exceptional talent. These roles range broadly from Talent Acquisition Specialists to Recruiting Coordinators and many in between. Understanding these roles, their responsibilities, and how they collaborate can shed light on the complex organism that is a talent acquisition team.

The meat and potatoes of a talent acquisition team are the Talent Acquisition Specialists. They handle the groundwork of identifying and engaging potential candidates, making them the backbone of the recruitment process. Specialists focus on understanding the hiring needs of the organization, crafting job descriptions, and promoting job ads. They also leverage their networks and various recruiting platforms to source potential candidates. If you love interacting with people and have a knack for assessing individuals' skills and potential, this role might be just your cup of tea.

Then we've got the Recruiting Coordinators. These unsung heroes of talent acquisition make sure all the gears in the recruitment machine are well-oiled and turning smoothly. Coordinators handle arrangements for interviews, manage communication between candidates and hiring managers, and work on the nitty-gritty details, like paperwork and administrative tasks. If you're detail-oriented, great at organizing, and love working behind the scenes to ensure a successful recruitment process, this could be the role for you.

The Talent Acquisition Managers are like the conductors of a bustling employment symphony. They oversee the recruitment process, set strategic objectives, manage the budget, monitor recruitment metrics, and work with hiring managers to understand and anticipate their departments' hiring needs. If you've got a strategic mind, leadership skills, and a comprehensive understanding of the recruitment process, this is where you'd shine.

In the role of Executive Search Consultant, the stakes are high. They're usually brought in to fill senior-level executive roles that have significant impact on the direction of the organization. This role requires a deep understanding of the industry, excellent networking skills, and the ability to assess high-level management and leadership skills. They're the star players invited on the field when the game is on the line!

Pretty much the Swiss Army knife of a talent acquisition team, the Sourcer is responsible for finding and attracting top-notch candidates. Sourcing involves utilizing various platforms and strategies to identify potential candidates who may not be actively seeking new opportunities. A Sourcer needs excellent research skills, creativity, and a solid understanding of the job market and industry trends.

Next up, we have Employer Brand Managers. These folks work hard to present the organization as a desirable place to work. They strategize and manage the employer's brand image, tailoring messaging to attract quality candidates who are a good cultural fit. If you've got a way with words, an understanding of branding, and an eye for what makes a company attractive, you'd fit right in.

Recently, we've seen the rise of another role: the Candidate Experience Manager. Their main objective? Ensuring that the recruitment process leaves a positive impression on all candidates, whether they're hired or not. This role requires excellent interpersonal skills, empathy, and a clear vision of how to offer a positive candidate experience.

Talent Acquisition Analysts, on the other hand, work with data to guide the recruitment process. They conduct analyses and report on recruitment metrics to help the team make informed decisions based on data, not just gut feelings. If you've got a knack for numbers, this could be your perfect match.

Remember the saying, "It takes a village to raise a child"? Well, it takes an equally diverse and dedicated team to attract, hire, and retain top talent. From Recruitment Marketing Specialists who lure candidates with engaging ads to HR Tech Specialists who ensure the seamless use of recruitment technologies, everyone has a crucial role to play.

Lastly, there's the Chief People Officer, nurturing the lifeblood of the organization—its people. This executive role oversees not only recruiting but also employee retention, workplace culture, and HR policies. A key player in the boardroom, they drive strategic initiatives that impact the company's talent acquisition and overall HR landscape.

So, now you've got the lowdown on some of the main roles in the talent acquisition field. Keep in mind, the specific tasks and responsibilities can vary based on the company's size, industry, and specific needs. However, these roles offer a solid understanding of the cogs in the talent acquisition machine and where your particular skills and interests may align.

No matter the role, everyone in talent acquisition aims to connect the right people with the right jobs. Each role is crucial, not just to the success of the talent acquisition process, but ultimately, to the success of the organization as a whole. So, if you're keen on building a career in this field, it's not just about where you will fit in, but also how your role will contribute to this bigger picture.

Because, at the end of the day, talent acquisition isn't just about filling vacancies—it's about finding the right people who'll drive the business forward. Different roles, with their unique responsibilities, work hand in hand to ensure this challenging, yet rewarding objective is met.

So, whether your thing is sourcing, branding, coordinating, analyzing, or managing—there's a place for you in the incredible world of talent acquisition. Here's to building a future where everyone can find their dream role, both within the talent acquisition team and beyond.

Components of Talent Acquisition

Continuing our journey into the world of talent acquisition, let's delve into its fundamental building blocks. Talent acquisition is the process of attracting, selecting, and onboarding skilled and qualified individuals for an organization. It's a fine art and science, blending together various aspects, like job analysis, recruitment strategies, candidate screening, and onboarding methods.

One of the first and most crucial components of talent acquisition is understanding the needs of the organization. An in-depth go through of the job description is a must to understand the skills, knowledge, and attributes required for the job. Hence, job analysis plays a vital role in giving direction to the talent acquisition process.

Next, planning recruitment strategies comes into play. Talent acquisition is all about being proactive rather than reactive. This means building a talent pipeline, ensuring a pool of talent is always at hand when vacancies arise. Here, sourcing and networking stand as meaningful areas of action, where recruiters build relationships with potential candidates, other professionals in their field, or past applicants to ensure a steady stream of potential applicants.

Once a pool of candidates gets created, screening begins. Some of the primary ways of doing this are examining resumes, conducting interviews, and various tests. Recruiters carry out these actions to ensure only the finest and most suitable applicants proceed further in the process.

Assessment is an integral part of talent acquisition. The application of psychometric assessments, skill-based tests, and behavioral interviews attempt to predict job performance. Combined, these tools can provide a well-rounded view of the candidate, giving sentiments of their abilities in the workplace.

Modern technology plays an increasingly vital role in talent acquisition, as well. Leveraging Applicant Tracking Systems (ATS) and Human Recourse Information Systems (HRIS) can streamline the process, making it quicker and more efficient. These systems can aid in sorting applications, scheduling interviews, and managing candidate databases.

Another key component is employment branding. A company's image significantly affects its ability to attract and retain high-quality employees. Therefore, developing a strong, positive employer brand is an essential part of talent acquisition. This means portraying the company as an attractive and favorable place to work, both internally and externally.

Further, a well-planned onboarding process is equally important. It's the company's chance to offer an enriching experience to the new hires, thoroughly integrating them into their new work environment. Done right, it can help the new employees adjust smoothly and make them feel valued, driving them to be more productive and loyal.

Building a diverse workforce is also part and parcel of talent acquisition. It adds dimensions of different cultures, languages, and viewpoints to the mix, leading to an environment rich in innovative ideas and approaches.

In addition, leveraging social media platforms for recruitment forms an equally crucial component of the talent acquisition process. With most of the world on social media today, it has become a goldmine for recruitment, allowing organizations to reach a broad audience and benefiting from relatively low costs.

Moreover, legal compliance cannot be overlooked. Laws and regulations related to hiring and employment should always be followed. Non-compliance can lead to costly penalties and could potentially harm the organization's reputation.

Yet another critical element is providing a great candidate experience. From application to onboarding, ensuring smooth interactions and transparent communication with candidates is vital. If the applicants feel respected and valued, they are more likely to accept job offers and speak highly of the company, even if they aren't selected, thus impacting future recruitments positively.

The final but equally significant ingredient to talent acquisition is a continuous improvement framework. Collecting feedback from candidates and hiring managers, data-driven decision-making, and always being on the lookout for the latest trends and best practices are critical to the constant evolution and improvement of the whole process. In addition, measuring key metrics like time-to-hire, cost-per-hire, and quality of hire can help track the efficiency of the talent acquisition strategy.

In conclusion, talent acquisition is a multifaceted process, playing a vital role in the organization's growth and success. Understanding these fundamental components and how they intertwine can help professionals in this field execute their work better and contribute significantly to their organizations' progress.

With the necessary components of talent acquisition now clear, our next chapter will highlight the organizational models in recruitment, bridging theory with practical workflows and structural configurations within talent acquisition teams.

Organizational Models in Recruiting

Continuing from our previous discussions, let's shift our focus onto the importance of organizational models in recruitment. Recruiting is an intricate process that goes beyond finding people to fit roles; it is about finding the right people at the right time in the right places. Different types of organizations use different models of recruiting based on their needs, sizes, and budgets.

One popular model is the centralized organizational model. In this setup, an organization maintains a singular, central recruiting team that takes care of all hiring needs across all departments. This guarantees consistency in hiring practices and policies, promotes effective use of resources, and fosters an overall unity in the recruitment approach.

But like anything else in business, the centralized model isn't without shortcomings. One key challenge is that it can potentially lead to a disconnect between the central recruitment team and the rest of the organization. This can lead to occasional misunderstandings of the specific hiring needs and requisites of individual departments.

Now let's hop over to the other end of the spectrum: the decentralized model. Here, each department within an organization manages its recruitment. Specialist recruiters with in-depth knowledge of their specific domain would understand their department's needs better and can make more informed decisions regarding hiring.

However, this hands-on, individual approach can lead to duplication of efforts, misalignment of goals, and inconsistent hiring practices. It might also lead to competition amongst departments for resources, creating granular challenges within the organization's structure.

Hybrid models, on the other hand, attempt to tap into the best of both worlds. Combining elements of both centralized and decentralized recruitment models, hybrid models aim at achieving a healthy balance between uniformity and flexibility. These models call for a central HR function aided by recruitment specialists in each department.

The coexistence of a central and decentral unit means there's a clear, unified strategy combined with a strong understanding of individual departmental needs. It, however, demands excellent communication and coordination to prevent any slippage between the gears.

Another interesting model is the recruitment process outsourcing (RPO) model, where an external provider is brought in to manage an organization's recruitment. This can provide scalability, cost-effectiveness, and access to best-practice processes and technology. But it also involves surrendering control of the recruitment process to the external provider, which might not resonate with all organizations.

Moving on, we find the in-house agency model. This involves creating a team within the organization that functions like an external recruitment agency. They use sales and marketing techniques to attract and engage candidates, offering an enhanced candidate experience. The challenge lies in building, maintaining, and resourcing such a team within the organization.

For many organizations, the recruitment model they adopt is contingent on various factors like size, sector, culture, and even location. A start-up might benefit from a centralized structure, while an MNC spread across multiple continents might prefer a decentralized or hybrid approach.

But remember, it's not enough to just pick a model and stick to it. Rigidity has no place in recruitment. A model needs to adapt and evolve as the organization grows and changes. So ongoing analysis and optimization are just as crucial as choosing the right model at the outset.

It's worth noting that with the rise of digital technology, the recruiting landscape is shifting. Implementing analytics and AI into recruitment practices can drastically improve the efficiency of an organization's model, regardless of its type.

Whatever model you adopt, it is crucial to ensure that it is aligned with the overall business strategy and enhances the candidate journey. The recruitment model should not just be about filling vacancies, but about driving business success through strategic talent acquisition.

In short, there is no one-size-fits-all strategy when it comes to recruitment models. It's a mix and match situation. Use your organizational context as a guide, consider your constraints and opportunities, and handpick a model that best suits you. Because at the end of the day, it's about getting the right people onboard to drive forward your organizational goals.

Up next, we'll take a closer look at the workflows in talent acquisition, understanding how the elements of recruitment come together in practice. So, shall we proceed?

Workflow in Talent Acquisition

Talent acquisition is more than just surfing through resumes and conducting interviews. It's a process, a flow of events that must be skillfully managed. The workflow in talent acquisition involves mapping out the entire process, from the moment a department identifies a need until a new hire is fully settled into the workplace.

This systematic workflow usually begins with understanding the job requirement. The hiring manager communicates the required skills, qualifications, and experience for the job. This step is vital – you could waste lots of time and resources if you don't get this right! Even worse, you could end up selecting a candidate that isn't the right fit for the role.

Once the job requirement is understood, it's time to map out a sourcing strategy. This involves deciding on the platforms to advertise the job opening, such as job boards, LinkedIn, and company websites.

Remember, a key part of talent acquisition is reaching out to quality candidates where they are most comfortable.

After sourcing, the application and screening process begins. Incoming resumes are sorted based on the outlined job requirements. Advanced application tracking systems (ATS) can assist in this process, with built-in AI helping to filter suitable candidates from the pile.

The next step, interviewing, is an essential part of the process. It's not just about fact-checking the candidate's CV. Interviews offer the chance to evaluate the candidate's soft skills, personality, and cultural fit in the organization. Always remember, the best talent often possesses the right blend of not just technical skills, but soft skills as well.

Upon identifying the potential candidate, the hiring manager and other decision-makers need to discuss and agree on the selection. Caution, diplomacy, and consensus play a significant role here – there's nothing worse than a new hire that the team doesn't believe in!

When the agreement is reached, the offer is made to the selected candidate. This part can be somewhat tricky, as it involves negotiation. But don't fret; a fair offer that balances the candidate's value and the company's budget typically wins the day.

Here's a key point: the workflow doesn't end with the signed job offer. Once the candidate accepts the offer, onboarding becomes the next vital step. A well-structured onboarding program helps new hires adapt quickly to the organization and their new role.

One thing to remember is that a well-laid workflow in talent acquisition hinges on two factors: efficiency and effectiveness. You don't want to waste time on unnecessary steps, but you also don't want to gloss over the essential parts of the process.

Efficiency is about speed and reducing costs. It's about leveraging technology like AI and ATS to streamline the process. But don't get too carried away with fast-tracking the process. Cutting corners can lead to poor quality hires, and that's a cost you don't want to bear.

Effectiveness, on the other hand, is about making sure you aren't just filling vacancies, but filling them with the right people. This implies that every step in the workflow is done right. From understanding job requirements to onboarding, each step must contribute to selecting the best talent for your organization.

Undeniably, technology plays a crucial part in modern talent acquisition workflows. From AI-enabled job postings to virtual interviews, technology can enhance the efficiency and effectiveness of the workflow.

However, while technology is great, let's not forget the human touch is essential. After all, we're dealing with people, not machines. People skills, especially communication and interpersonal relations, are key to every talent acquisition process.

The workflow in talent acquisition is complex, yet rewarding. When done correctly, it's a sure-fire way to attract and retain the best talent. Keep in mind, the end goal is not to have a 'perfect' process, but rather a process that continually evolves and improves. With a well-defined workflow and a focus on both efficiency and effectiveness, your talent acquisition process will be in a league of its own.

Building a Talent Acquisition Function

Building a Talent Acquisition function doesn't happen overnight—it's a gradual process that requires strategy, planning, and ongoing attention. It's a bit like constructing a complex building; you need a solid foundation, a detailed blueprint, and the right tools for the job. Once you have all these elements, it becomes a matter of skillfully putting everything together.

For starters, let's focus on the 'foundation'. The first step in building a Talent Acquisition function is to understand your organization's needs. This means getting a solid understanding of the company's goals, mission, and culture. The more you know about your organization, the more you're able to align the Talent Acquisition function with its strategic direction.

Next, you need to craft a clear talent acquisition strategy. This strategy is your 'blueprint'. It should outline what types of roles you're looking to fill, what skills are needed, when and where to source candidates, how to screen and interview candidates, and how to retain top talent. Each step should be clearly defined and easily understood by everyone involved in the process.

Once the strategy is in place, it's time to decide on the 'tools'. In the 21st century, this often translates to technology. There's a myriad of tech tools available for sourcing, recruitment, and applicant tracking. But remember, the technology is just a tool; it's the people using these tools that make the real difference. Therefore, consider your team's skills and comfort level with technology during the selection process.

A key point to remember is that a Talent Acquisition Function isn't a standalone entity—it deeply interacts with different teams within an organization. For example, your talent acquisition strategy must reflect the needs expressed by the hiring managers and should be in sync with the principles and goals of the HR department. Inclusion and cooperation are the name of the game here.

Another critical part of building a Talent Acquisition function is deciding on its structure. This could mean choosing between a centralized approach, where all recruiting activities are handled by a single team, or a decentralized approach, where various departments have their dedicated recruiters. Deciding on the right structure often involves considering the size of the company, the nature of the roles, and team expertise.

Training and development form an important part of building a robust Talent Acquisition function. Even the best Talent Acquisition professionals need to continuously upskill and reskill to keep up with market trends. Regular workshops and training programs can help team members stay at the top of their game.

The task of identifying and acquiring talent doesn't end at hire. After a successful recruitment, it's important to set up a seamless onboarding process. This process helps new hires adjust to the company culture and their new roles faster, leading to improved productivity and reduced turnover.

When building the function, one must also remember to incorporate a system for performance measurement. Key Performance Indicators (KPIs) should be defined to track and measure the success of your acquisition function. These KPIs could include metrics such as time-to-hire, cost-per-hire, quality of hire, and retention rates.

The task of building a Talent Acquisition function can seem overwhelming. However, repeated experimentation, learning, and optimization are part of the process. Do not get disheartened by initial failures or challenges. Cultivating an agile mindset where you consider these roadblocks as a path to improvement can be a game-changer.

Note that it's not just the building – it's also about maintaining and evolving. Even after a successful Talent Acquisition function is in place, it needs to be examined and updated regularly for relevancy and efficiency. Monitoring current hiring trends is a must, as it helps you attract and retain top talent successfully.

Finally, remember that the core of Talent Acquisition lies in relationships: between recruiters, hiring managers, candidates, and employees. Building a fruitful Talent Acquisition function is, in large part, about nurturing those relationships for mutual benefit.

In the following chapters, we'll delve into the nuts and bolts of sourcing, attracting, engaging, and assessing candidates. Like any skill, the art of Talent Acquisition can be mastered with practice, tenacity, and a bit of creativity. So, let's jump right in and learn all about crafting an exceptional Talent Acquisition function!

Chapter 1:
Define

Stepping into the realm of talent acquisition is like dipping your toes into an ocean of possibilities, it's complex yet endlessly fascinating. Imagine it as a strategic game of chess, with you making moves to outwit your competition and acquire the right talent. Now, you're probably like "Wait, I thought hiring was just about filling positions?" Well, it's so much more than that. Talent acquisition isn't just about finding people to plug gaps; it's about proactively seeking top-notch professionals who can drive an organization forward. As we delve deeper into this chapter, you'll find that sourcing is an art and recruitment is a strategic science amalgamating recommendations on building the function. You'll soon begin to perceive how the recruitment process is like a well-oiled machine; each gear representing a different function, turning to drive the mechanism forward. But before you dive headlong into this unraveling adventure, it's time to set some definitions straight. Clear and concise understanding forms the keystone to successful application, and that's exactly what we aim to foster here. So let's first comprehend what sourcing and recruitment truly entail, and how building this function strategically plays a significant role in successful talent acquisition.

Introduction to Sourcing

When diving into talent acquisition and recruitment, there's a term you can't skip - Sourcing. It's almost like the secret sauce that makes the recruitment process successful. Akin to finding a needle in a haystack, sourcing is the art and science of identifying and attracting potential candidates. In simple terms, sourcing involves finding the right person, for the right job, at the right time.

Before you start thinking that sourcing is just another fancy term for recruitment, let's clarify. Yes, sourcing is a part of the recruitment process but is a distinctive function in itself. Logically speaking, you can't recruit if you don't have someone to recruit, right? That's where sourcing comes in. It's the early stage of any recruitment process that focuses solely on identifying potential candidates, even before a job is open.

Sourcing can't be done haphazardly. It requires a dependable and repeatable process derived from a blend of active and passive strategies. Active sourcing methods involve direct outreach to candidates, like sending messages via LinkedIn or emails. On the flip side, passive sourcing involves creating a strong employer brand that attracts candidates naturally over time.

Also, not all roles are created equal. Some roles are easier to fill than others. This means your sourcing strategy must be adaptable and flexible. Adaptability in sourcing allows effective adjusting to different talent landscapes. When it comes to roles that are harder to fill, the methodology and complexity of sourcing becomes critical.

If you are under the impression that sourcing is a one-man job, think again. Sourcing is a team game. It involves collaboration between various people like the hiring manager, the recruitment team, and sometimes even the team the candidate would join. Everyone has a part to play, from understanding the role requirements to tracking down potential candidates, to creating a seamless hiring experience.

Everything that has been covered so far may seem overwhelming at first. But sourcing is not just about crazy amounts of information and complicated jargon. It's also an opportunity to be creative and innovative, to really rethink how recruitment is done.

Choosing the right sourcing techniques is vital. Different situations call for various approaches. Some candidates might not be active on job boards but are active on social media platforms. Others might be reached better through professional networks or events. Researching where potential candidates spend their time and how best to connect with them is essential in sourcing.

In addition, tech-savvy sourcing is of considerable importance these days. With modern technology at our fingertips, sourcing can become smarter. Artificial Intelligence, Machine Learning, and predictive analytics can help recruiters sift through heaps of data to find potential candidates.

Another vital thing to remember in sourcing is the importance of building relationships with potential candidates. Sourcing is not just about finding candidates; it's about being a good listener, communicator, manager, and marketer. Nurturing these relationships can often help you get future hires, even if the person is not active in the job market at that moment.

Finally, one could argue that the goal of sourcing extends beyond merely filling a current role. It's about creating diverse talent pools that can help the company fulfill its present and future hiring needs. This aids in decreasing the hiring time, as when a position becomes available, a pre-qualified group of candidates already exist from which to draw.

In conclusion, sourcing is the foundation of any successful recruitment process. It's an advanced methodology requiring specific skills, creativity, adaptability, and an understanding of modern technology trends. Despite the challenges it brings, sourcing presents a thrilling opportunity to transform the way companies hire and expand their teams.

As we venture ahead in the chapters, we'll delve deeper into the techniques and tactics of sourcing. We'll discuss how to utilize different searching methodologies, innovative sourcing techniques, and even international recruiting. This world is waiting for you to discover, so let's dive deeper and make you a real sourcing ninja.

Overview of Recruitment

So, what exactly is recruitment? Just to set the stage, picture it as a kind of matchmaking. It's not merely about hiring people for job positions, but about finding the right fit for the job and the organization. It's about identifying and attracting potential candidates, assessing their capabilities and skills, and ultimately selecting the ideal candidate. This isn't simply about ticking boxes; it entails a lot more finesse and strategic planning than you might imagine.

Discussing recruitment in broad terms, it's essentially a two-step process. Think of it like a dance. First, you have the identification phase, in which you identify the potential candidates who fit your job criteria. This could be in terms of experience, qualifications, skills, or even personality traits. Next is the selection phase, where the identified candidates go through various selection methods, such as interviews, tasks, or assessments, to determine who is the most suitable for the job.

But let's dive a little deeper. In the first phase, you not only identify possible candidates, but you also seek to attract them to your organization. You have to make them see your organization as a place where they would want to work. You've got to be persuasive, selling the organization's culture, values, benefits, and so on. Sometimes this requires a little creativity and out-of-the-box thinking to make your company stand out from the crowd.

In the selection process, the focus shifts to evaluating the candidates. You sort through applications, conduct interviews, and carry out assessments. You're drawing a clearer picture of who these candidates are, their skills, experience, and their potential fit in the organization. It's like playing detective, sleuthing out the clues to identify who might be the right person for the task at hand.

A crucial aspect of recruitment is communication. We're talking about access to quality and timely information for all involved parties. The lines of communication should always remain open, ensuring transparency, reducing tension and making the entire process run smoothly. This could be from setting clear expectations, providing updates, giving feedback, or addressing possible concerns.

And, like any strategy worth its salt, recruitment isn't static. It's dynamic, it's fluid. You need to pay attention to shifts in industry trends, changes in business strategy, or even modifications in specific job roles. You might need to revise your recruitment processes, methodologies, and even tools used to stay in tune with these changes. So, it requires constant monitoring, and yes, a little wiggle-room for adaptability.

Moreover, we must always consider the impact of technology in recruitment. In the current digital era, almost every aspect of our lives has been influenced by technology, and recruitment is no exception. There's a vast array of digital tools and platforms that can assist recruiters in their quest to find the perfect candidate. From job boards and applicant tracking systems to social media and artificial intelligence, technology can transform and enhance your recruitment strategies.

Furthermore, recruitment doesn't end with hiring. In many ways, it's just the beginning. Once the candidate is on-board, it's crucial to ensure their smooth transition into the role and the organization. Remember, the aim is to create a positive candidate experience, reinforcing the organization's employer brand.

And not to forget, recruitment is a vital component of a larger umbrella known as talent acquisition. Although both terms are often used interchangeably, talent acquisition is significantly broader, encompassing other elements like succession planning, targeted headhunting, and talent relationship management. It's a long-term strategy intricately linked to the organization's strategic goals.

Whatever the size or scope of the organization, recruitment plays a crucial role in its success. An organization's greatest asset is its people, and thus, hiring the right talent is critical. Wrong hiring decisions can have significant consequences, impacting productivity, team morale, and even financial performance. Hence, effective recruitment is more than just an operational necessity; it also possesses a strategic dimension.

Last but not least, remember that recruitment isn't a solo endeavor. It's a team effort involving recruiters, hiring managers, senior managers, and even current employees. Each plays a critical role in the recruitment dance, contributing to the formation of a competent, dynamic, and productive workforce.

So, there we have it, folks. To sum up, recruitment is a dance, a matchmaking process that involves identifying, attracting, evaluating, and selecting candidates. It's a dynamic, fluid process that requires clear communication, technology, adaptability, and a strategic approach. And above all, it's a cooperative effort that contributes to the very lifeblood of the organization—its talent.

Strategic Recommendations on Building the Function

Talent acquisition is not merely about filling vacancies; it's about strategically finding and attracting the best talent to meet organizational goals. The best place to start? By defining your objectives and crafting a blueprint for your function. So let's dive into some strategic recommendations for building a robust talent acquisition function.

First things first, it's critical to understand your organization's goals and needs. Every company has unique needs, and the talent acquisition function should align with those. Aligning recruitment with your organization's goals can streamline the process, ensuring that the right talent is found for the right roles. This way, the talent acquired will not just be employees filling roles but an essential part of the company's strategic direction.

Next, consider the resources at your disposal. Like everything else in business, effective talent acquisition requires investment. The budget will influence the size of your recruitment team, the technology you can afford, and the networks you can build. While it can be tough to balance the budget against needs, keep in mind that skimping out now can lead to higher costs later in the form of poor hires or vacancies that take longer to fill.

Speaking of teams, the individuals who make up your talent acquisition team can significantly impact the function's success. Having a mix of skill sets and backgrounds can lead to more innovative strategies and attract diverse talent. Recognize your team's strengths, provide training where needed, and don't forget to nurture a positive and supportive atmosphere.

We're living in the digital age, so ignoring technology isn't an option. Consider the technology you need for successful talent acquisition. This could be anything from applicant tracking systems to video interviewing software. Leveraging technology not only speeds up the hiring process but provides valuable data that can help improve future recruitment efforts. However, be mindful of not letting technology replace the human touch— a balance is key.

A successful talent acquisition strategy also means understanding and developing the Employer Value Proposition (EVP). A strong EVP can be the magnet that attracts top talent. It's the unique set of benefits and opportunities employees experience working within your organization. Craft an attractive and authentic EVP, and it can be a game-changer for your talent acquisition efforts.

Next on the list is establishing a robust sourcing strategy. Sourcing is a pro-active recruitment method that involves identifying and engaging talent before a vacancy appears. This means cultivating relationships and establishing a talent pipeline for future positions.

Creative sourcing methods can provide a competitive advantage in the talent market.

Building a strong employer brand is another crucial step. Your employer brand is the company's image - it's what attracts job seekers and keeps employees loyal. A recognizable, positive employer brand can be the difference between attracting top-tier talent and struggling to fill vacancies.

Once you've attracted talent, it's equally important to engage them. Engagement isn't just about selling the role or the company; it's about building a genuine relationship. It includes clear communication, regular updates, and a hiring process that respects the candidate's time and effort.

The metrics you choose to evaluate your recruitment efforts can shape the future success of your talent acquisition function. Utilize data-driven decision-making to assess what's working and what isn't. From time-to-fill, cost-per-hire, to quality-of-hire, selecting relevant metrics can provide invaluable insights into your talent acquisition function.

Equally important is to not overlook diversity and inclusion elements. Having diverse employees brings an array of perspectives and skills, promoting creativity and innovation. An inclusive recruitment process seeks out this diversity, highlighting your organization as a place open and accommodating to all.

If your organization operates in multiple countries, remember that talent acquisition isn't a one-size-fits-all process. Different regions can mean different employment laws, cultural norms, and candidate expectations. Thus, a localized recruitment strategy may be more effective when operating internationally.

Lastly, always be ready to adapt. The world of talent acquisition is continually evolving, with new tools, techniques, and expectations changing the game. Being open to change and prepared to adjust your strategies can keep your talent acquisition function ahead of the curve.

To sum up, building a strategic talent acquisition function requires a comprehensive understanding of your organization's vision, a well-equipped team, savvy use of technology, and a strong employer brand. Throw in a focus on diversity and the flexibility to adapt, and you've got yourself a winning strategy.

This chapter has focused on recommendations for building an effective talent acquisition function. The subsequent chapters will delve into the processes of finding, attracting and engaging talent, and finally achieving successful implementation of these activities. Let this form the foundation of what's to come in your talent acquisition journey.

Chapter 2:
Find - Comprehensive Examination of Talent Identification Techniques

Drilling down into the crux of talent acquisition, let's crack open the realm of the various talent identification techniques. Like a gold prospector seeking the precious metal, the challenge isn't just to find candidates—it's about sifting the nuggets from the dirt. It's both an art and a science that morphs with the advent of new methods and technologies. Traditional search methods are still valuable, of course. We're talking about job postings, internal databases, staffing agencies, et cetera. But in the digital age, we're not limited to these conventional paths. There's potential in every corner—the internet, for example, presents a voluminous, yet challenging, resource for passive candidates. Harnessing this resource requires adaptability and a grasp of varying methodologies, right from Boolean searches to complex web scraping techniques.

But we can't ignore kicker strategies like referral sourcing, peer regression, and social recruiting. These are innovative alternatives that challenge traditional norms and push us to think outside the box. And it doesn't stop there! If we look broader, international recruiting ventures into uncharted territory crossing cultural and geographical borders. You'll do well to remember though—these techniques aren't a one-size-fits-all solution. Each organization, or even job role for that matter, might require a different approach. Talent identification then becomes a fascinating jigsaw puzzle where you're constantly reconfiguring techniques to find the perfect fit. And trust me, when you find that right person for the job, it feels like hitting a bullseye!

Internet Search for Passive Candidates

Next on our talent hunt is the internet search for passive candidates. These are not the people enthusiastically typing up job applications, but rather, professionals who are open to new opportunities, even if they aren't actively seeking them. The internet, with its vast reservoirs of data and information, provides an immense asset in unearthing these valuable targets.

So, the question arises, how can we leverage this online gold mine to locate passive candidates? Well, we roll up our sleeves, put on our digital detective hats, and delve into the powers of search engines. But it's not your run-of-the-mill Google search we're talking about here. Advanced search techniques utilizing targeted keywords, phrases, and other specific criteria can draw a bead on potential candidates lurking in the deep web corners.

Alright, let's dive a bit deeper. Say for instance, you need a UX designer. You'd start by plugging in the keywords "**UX designer**". Too broad? Throw in attributes like a particular skill level, specific industry experience, or even geographical location. These additional filters bring us one step closer to our desired candidate.

Increasing the effectiveness of our search, boolean operators step onto stage. These allow us to join or exclude keywords, creating a far more specific search query. Combining these in the right way can truly bolster your efforts in unearthing passive candidates.

Let's not limit ourselves to just search engines. Niche job boards, industry-specific forums, online communities, and professional networking sites such as LinkedIn offer robust platforms to track down prospective candidates. The more you understand the landscape and culture of these online spaces, the more effective you'll be in finding the proverbial needle in the haystack.

If you're after senior-level or highly specialized talent, sites like GitHub for coders and Behance for designers serve as treasure troves. On these platforms, professionals not only list their skills and experience, but frequently showcase their portfolios as well. This means you get more than just a snapshot of their work history, you can see the quality of their work firsthand.

Remember one important thing here, passive candidates don't display an 'I'm available' sign. This means you need to be sharp-eyed. Pick up on indicators like their involvement in professional communities or feedback they've provided on industry-related topics. These acts often signal a certain restlessness and openness to fresh prospects.

By now, you might be thinking it all sounds like a colossal task. And you're right. Manually sifting through pages of search results is anything but exhilarating. That's where advanced search technologies come into play, automating the process and saving you valuable time.

Candidate sourcing technologies use AI-powered algorithms to scour data from a range of sources, building a comprehensive candidate profile. Some even rank candidates based on the match between your specifications and their profile. This approach significantly reduces the time and effort involved in locating potential matches.

Now, discovery is one thing, engagement is another. Finding passive candidates won't mean much if you can't get their attention. That's where your communication strategy steps in. Soft-sell, personalised emails that engage on a professional level often work well. However, keep an open mind and try varied approaches to figure out which works best for your target segment.

Before we wrap up, let's not overlook the human aspect in all this tech-driven chasing. As you reach out to these passive candidates, remember, they're not job seekers in the traditional sense. They're not desperate for a job, you are trying to lure them away from their comfort zone. The interaction must be mutually beneficial and respectful.

Internet search for passive candidates can unarguably be a demanding task. It requires a balance of technical savvy, personal touch, and intuition. It also requires a hefty investment of time, as nurturing these relationships is key to successful outcomes.

This approach, while demanding, offers a unique advantage in talent acquisition. It helps connect with professionals who might not otherwise be in your candidate pool and offers vastly expanded possibilities. Building this capability is an investment that can significantly boost your talent acquisition efforts.

There we have it. Internet search for passive candidates is one of those lesser-used channels in talent identification, but carried out effectively, it can be a goldmine. Don't be daunted by the vastness of the internet; remember, the right candidate is out there. All you need is the right combination of strategies and patience to find them.

Utilizing Various Methodologies

Having sifted through the vast realms of the internet in pursuit of the perfect talent, it's crucial to approach the resultant data with a structured methodology. We're not looking to reinvent the wheel here. We're simply drawing from existing methodologies, tweaking them a tad bit to devise a systematic approach which can deal with the fluid nature of this profession.

The first methodology that deserves mention is the tried-and-true Boolean search. It's revered for its precision, bringing back results that are exactly what was input. That's because Boolean searches require operators like 'AND,' 'OR,' or 'NOT' to sift through varied sources to draw up a refined list of potential candidates. But remember, Boolean isn't a magic trick! You've got to learn the ropes, gain an understanding of its syntax and potential - it takes practice, but the results are more than worth it.

Speaking of practice makes perfect, we have semantic search methodologies. Where Boolean is a word for word matchmaker, semantics takes context into account, playing matchmaker on the basis of relevance. This is where algorithms flex their muscles, and machine learning models fine-tune search results. Naturally, this method proves beneficial when we're dealing with diverse candidate profiles and job specifications. Remember, while you let technology do the heavy lifting, it's crucial you maintain the driver's seat, refining the search parameters as you go along.

Familiar with deemed associations? Then you're not new to relationship sourcing. This is the byword for making connections and exploring networks to identify candidates. LinkedIn is a gold mine for this, especially with the 'People Also Viewed' and 'People You May Know' features. But don't limit yourself to LinkedIn. Facebook, Instagram and even Twitter can reveal surprising connections, so keep explorative networking on your radar.

Then there's advanced sourcing, or what we can call the 'deep dive.' It's about finding hidden gems in places where most people wouldn't bother looking. Scraping through discussion forums or professional communities may seem tedious, but it's exactly where you could find that needle in the haystack. Keeping an eye on industry-specific forums, community threads and even comment sections can reveal impressive talents often overlooked by others.

There's also the 'persona' driven methodology or what we like to call 'peer regression.' It's about understanding the character sketch of an ideal candidate and gearing our search engine to filter candidates falling in the same bracket. Breaking the broader role down into specific personas enables a more targeted search, and a well-defined persona can be a treasure trove of leads.

Let's not forget the passive prospect search. Too often, recruiters overlook those folks who aren't actively looking for a job but could be the perfect fit. Effective utilization of talent databases can turn dormant profiles into active candidates. Job boards, resume databases, and LinkedIn Pro can be beneficial in such scenarios.

Parallel to all this, ensure you're also on the look-out for referrals because let's face it, they're still one of the strongest talent identification techniques. Your talents aren't just employees, they're brand ambassadors with the power of 'in-network' tacit endorsements. Leverage this; you'll be surprised at the quality of talent they can channel right to your doorstep.

As you delve deeper, you'll realize there's no 'one size fits all' in this field. Different roles require different search methodologies. For instance, creative roles might require a completely different approach, requiring you to dive into portfolio websites like Behance or Dribbble, service marketplaces like Upwork or Freelancer, or even social media platforms like Instagram.

Despite the exhaustive nature of your search, remember to approach it all with a level-headedness. Talent identification is as much about being patient and methodical as it is about speed and efficiency. Balanced persistence is key.

The true beauty of recruitment lies in its merging of art and science. Utilization of varied methodologies reinforces this. Be it exploring Boolean search's binary prowess, semantic search's contextual wisdom, connecting through relationship sourcing, deep-diving with advanced sourcing, creating archetypes through persona-based search, or tapping into the gold mine of passive candidate databases, use these techniques as tools to shape your recruitment canvas. Each tool paints a different part of the picture. It's not just about the analytics and metrics, it's about putting those human instincts at work and connecting the dots like a pro.

So now, as you move forward, think of these methodologies as not just talent identification techniques, but as sculpting tools in your recruitment arsenal. We might be looking for talent in a digital age, but our processes mustn't lose the human touch that defines our roles.

Our journey as recruiters is all about constant learning and adapting. Yes, there will be challenges and roadblocks. Sometimes, indexed or stored data may lead nowhere, the perfect Boolean string might return zero results, and the ideal candidate might not actually exist. But remember, each stumbling block is merely a stepping stone towards refining your talent identification skills further.

At the end of the day, both recruiters and candidates are on the same boat, navigating the choppy waters of the recruitment sea. Our collective efforts can make these waters less daunting, making the candidate experience smoother than ever and our search more successful. Here's to mastering the art of detective pursuit within recruitment, and employing a range of methodologies to find the perfect fit. Looking forward to meeting the techniques touched upon in the following chapters. Until then, happy recruiting!

Innovative Search Techniques: Natural Language

As we continue exploring talent identification techniques, we will delve into a truly groundbreaking approach: natural language processing. The field of talent acquisition is continually evolving, and natural language search techniques are a testament to that relentless progress. So, what's all the fuss about this cutting-edge tool?

Well, simply put, natural language processing, commonly known as NLP, is a subset of artificial intelligence. It is focused on building systems that understand and interact with humans in a natural, human-like manner. NLP promises to redefine traditional prospecting by allowing recruiters to search for candidates using regular language, as opposed to relying on specific keywords or complex Boolean queries.

Imagine being able to type, "I need a software developer with five years of JavaScript experience" into your recruiting software, and it immediately pulls up a list of suitable candidates. That's the kind of simplicity and efficiency we're talking about. This approach eliminates the need for complex searches and allows recruiters to find top-tier candidates easier and faster.

But don't just take our word for it. Let's delve into why natural language processing could be a goldmine for recruiters.

Firstly, NLP technology goes beyond simple pattern recognition. It doesn't just match keywords in a resume to the ones in the job description. It understands the context and semantic intricacies of human language and accordingly fetches nuanced information from candidate profiles.

Secondly, it offers broader search possibilities. Instead of needing to know specific search operators or syntax, recruiters can use everyday language. This allows individuals with varied linguistic skills to participate actively in candidate search and identification.

Thirdly, NLP technology allows for more nuanced filtering of candidate profiles. Think of it as having sincere and meaningful conversations with each document or profile and ascertaining whether they might be right for a role. It's not just about ticking boxes; it's about understanding the candidate in a more holistic way.

That said, let's not sweep the potential challenges under the carpet. Yes, implementing NLP requires considerable setup and preparation. Business processes may need to be altered, and staff may need to be trained to handle new technologies. It will be important to have technical support at the ready to deal with any unexpected hiccups that might occur.

Another thing to consider is the quality of data. For the system to return meaningful results, it needs meaningful input. Garbage in, garbage out, as they say. Ensuring the quality of data input is of paramount importance.

Now, it's critical to understand that NLP shouldn't replace human recruiters. It's not about creating a robot that does the entire recruitment job for us. It's about enhancing and streamlining the process, freeing up recruiters to focus on building relationships and making strategic decisions.

The integration of NLP into talent acquisition signifies an exciting step forward. It points to a world where searching for candidates becomes as simple as using everyday language. Of course, there might be hurdles along the way, but the potential benefits are undeniable and too promising to ignore.

So there you have it, natural language search techniques. It's the future knocking at the door of talent acquisition, and it's high time we answered.

To conclude, remember this: natural language processing is an invaluable tool, but it's just that – a tool. The human touch will forever be the heart and soul of talent acquisition. But with powerful tools like NLP at our disposal, we can ensure our human efforts are better directed and more fruitful, morphing the world of talent acquisition into a more efficient and effective domain.

Innovative Search Techniques: Peer Regression

The talent acquisition arena is an ever-evolving field, and to stay ahead of the competition, embracing innovative search techniques and strategies is key. One such strategy is peer regression. Want to know more about this cutting-edge technique? Let's dive right into it.

Essentially, peer regression is a proactive talent identification technique, one that isn't as widely utilized as it should be. In a nutshell, it's about using the knowledge of an existing great hire to find more people who could potentially be just as good, if not better!

Taking a step back, remember how you found your best hires? Were they recommended by someone in your organization? Or did you stumble upon them on professional networking sites? Could it be possible to find more people like them? It's all about finding the common denominator, and regression techniques like these allow us to establish a pattern.

The base of a peer regression search technique is identifying the commonalities among your top performers, and then using that information to find similar candidates. It's not just about skills and experience - it's about seeing beyond the traditional resume spectrum.

What do your star employees have in common in terms of education, previous employers, roles, web presence, skills or interests? More often than not, there are patterns that emerge. For example, you might notice that your star performers all come from a handful of schools or specific roles within other organizations. This isn't a coincidence - it's a clue to where you can find similar talent.

When you've discovered a pattern, the next step is to use this insight to fuel your sourcing activities. It's like setting an algorithm into motion. You've identified certain proven markers of success; now it's time to base your search on these markers.

That being said, while peer regression can be a powerful tool, it's not an exact science, nor is it a foolproof method. It's simply a guide to help you narrow down a broad talent pool into something much more manageable and likely to yield quality results.

Note: It's crucial not to get caught in what's known as 'pattern bias.' Every organization has a unique culture, a unique set of operations and nuanced requirements for each role. Therefore, what works for one may not work for the other. A balanced approach is essential.

Peer regression is a strategy best implemented over time, alongside traditional methodologies. It's a bit like gardening. You plant a seed, nurture it, let it grow, but you also need to keep an eye on the weeds (ineffective sources) and pull them out before they overtake the healthy parts of your garden.

It's important to remember that peer regression, as with all sourcing strategies, is about more than just finding resumes. Its end goal is to uncover individuals who have the potential to succeed in your environment. It's about talent fit, contributing to the growth and success of your organization.

Finding high-potential candidates isn't easy; it's challenging work that requires a great deal of ingenuity and persistent effort. However, the utilization of innovative search techniques, such as peer regression, can significantly change the game.

It might sound a bit complex, but once you get the hang of it, you'll find that it's an incredibly useful tool in your arsenal. With the right kind of detailed, organized approach, you can use peer regression to find stellar candidates, making your job as a talent acquisition specialist that much easier – well, perhaps not easier, but certainly more effective.

So, have we got you nodding along, thinking about the potential of peer regression? That's what we like to hear! The key point to remember is that innovation is at the core of successful talent acquisition. It's not just about doing things differently – it's about doing things better. Dare to explore, innovate, and evolve. And remember, the best recruiters are those who are not afraid to take chances and embrace new techniques. Now, go forth and conquer!

Innovative Search Techniques: Referral Sourcing

Continuing on our exploration of Innovative Search Techniques, let's dive into a favorite sourcing strategy among recruiters - referral sourcing. Referral sourcing leverages the relationships of current employees, past employees, and external networks to source candidates for open positions.

There's a common saying in the recruitment world: "Good talent knows good talent". This principle is the driving force behind referral sourcing. People within your network or company are likely to know others who possess similar skills, qualities, or expertise. This innovative search technique can provide an advantageous talent pool that might otherwise be hidden or overlooked.

Why does this method work? First and foremost, referrals often come with a level of trust that is inherently attached. The recommender, most likely an employee or past employee, has first-hand knowledge of the company culture, work expectations, and job specifics. The chances that the recommended candidate will align with organizational objectives are significantly higher as the referrals are more likely to be a culture-fit.

Furthermore, referred candidates typically have a higher retention rate. The reassurance that the workplace has been vouched for by someone they trust encourages the candidate to stay longer, confirming the long-term effectiveness of referral sourcing.

Referral programs within organizations are common. These often offer incentives to employees for successful hires from their referrals. It only makes sense, right? After all, motivated employees will bring in a robust, talent-rich network that can be utilized now and in the future.

Oftentimes, recruiters actively encourage employees to introduce potential candidates not just from their professional network, but also from their personal networks. If a happy team member can effectively communicate the organization's core values and success stories, it can build a positive image that attracts prospective candidates.

While referral sourcing can produce excellent results, it's crucial to remember that it must be used in conjunction with other innovative search techniques. If relied on solely, referral sourcing can lead to a lack of diversity within the hiring pool. Talent acquisition professionals should weave this method into their recruiting strategy, blurring the lines between the traditional and the innovative.

To optimize referral sourcing, consider building a referral culture from the ground up. Encourage sharing and building networks from the outset, integrating referrals into every aspect of the recruitment process. One way to accomplish this is through consistent communication and education. It's essential that employees understand the types of candidates their organization is seeking, and the ideal cultural fit.

It's worth noting that the advent of social media has amplified the scope of referral sourcing. LinkedIn, for example, allows one to scrutinize the connections of employees, finding potential candidates who might otherwise have been overlooked. Utilizing these networks forms a compelling argument for incorporating digital networking tools into referral sourcing strategies.

Measurement and analytics play a critical role as well. Regular monitoring and reporting on the performance of the referral program can provide valuable insights. It's key to track the quantity and quality of referral leads, then adjust strategies as needed, ensuring a continuous improvement in the referral sourcing strategy.

All things considered, when done right, referral sourcing can significantly improve the quality of potential candidates, reduce recruitment costs, and enhance employee engagement. It's advisable for businesses to invest time in designing efficient referral programs, actively promoting them within their networks, and integrating them harmoniously with other, less traditional methods of candidate sourcing.

However, remember that referral sourcing, while a critical component, is just one piece of the talent acquisition puzzle. Its strength lies in its integration with other innovative search techniques. The most successful recruiters understand how to optimize for the mix, ensuring they aren't leaving any stone unturned in the tireless quest to find and attract top talent.

The following section will introduce another innovative search technique – social recruiting, which blends the traditional approach with digital methods to build a robust and diverse talent pipeline. Stick around, the journey on talent identification techniques is not over yet!

Innovative Search Techniques: Social Recruiting

The realm of talent acquisition has, in recent years, significantly revolutionized due to the rise of social recruiting. It's an exciting time as businesses are changing the way they source and connect with potential talents. For the uninitiated, social recruiting is the method of recruiting candidates by using social platforms as talent databases or for advertising.

LinkedIn, Facebook, and Twitter are generally the most popular platforms for recruiting, but don't ignore the potential of niche platforms and forums where potential candidates might hang out. By employing this innovative approach, companies are nourishing their employment brands while fostering meaningful relationships with potential candidates. At the same time, it allows sourcing professionals to observe potential candidates in an environment that often gives more holistic insight into their skills, values, and personality.

So, how does one dive into the world of social recruiting? Start by setting up professional accounts across multiple platforms. These are your tools for connecting with potential candidates, sharing your company's story, and reaching out to prospective talents. It's crucial, however, to ensure your messages encompass the brand's voice and mission.

Now you might be wondering: how can I find high-potential candidates on social platforms? It's simple: use the platforms' search feature and unspecified methods. You can use boolean searches, filter parameters, or utilize advanced search functions to find profiles that match your recruiting needs. Remember, your potential candidate might not be actively seeking a job, so scour the social networks for passive candidates too.

Engaging with candidates on social platforms isn't just about shooting them a message. It's about creating engaging content that interests them and prompts them to learn more about your company. You can't just spam potential candidates with job postings. It's essential to strike a balance between professional content and posts that showcase your company culture and values.

Another significant benefit of social recruiting is the ability to leverage your network. Connections matter in recruiting. Once you build relationships with candidates, they are more likely to recommend others in their network. It's a ripple effect that can yield excellent results. Make sure to always say 'Thanks!' to those who refer potential candidates. A little appreciative measure goes a long way.

A crucial thing to consider with social recruiting is responsiveness. As recruiters, maintain an open line of communication with potential candidates. When someone reaches out or shows interest, immediate engagement is vital to represent your brand and move forward with potential talents promptly.

The beauty of social recruiting lies in its informality and conversational approach. Here, it is pivotal to sprinkle some human elements into your engagement. By expressing authenticity in your outreach, it allows the potential candidates to visualize themselves in your organization.

As a recruiter, it is valuable to consider diversity while scouting on social media platforms. Representation matters, and it is essential to ensure your talent pool is diverse in terms of race, gender, age, abilities, and other aspects. Social recruiting provides a broad platform to engage with prospects from varied backgrounds and experiences, enhancing the richness of your talent pool.

Importantly, social recruiting should merge harmoniously with other recruiting strategies. It makes for a stronger, all-inclusive recruiting strategy when combined with other traditional recruitment methods. Exclusively relying on social recruiting isn't recommended as it might catch you off guard by the ever-changing social media algorithms and trends. That's why, to unlock its full potential, blend social recruiting with other methods.

Sure, navigating the waters of social recruiting might seem a little daunting. But remember, it's not just about putting a tick on a box. It's about optimizing a tool that already exists - social media. When done right, you are forging connections, expressing your brand ideologies, and tapping into a resourceful talent-pool.

Let's be clear: social recruiting isn't just a fad; it's here to stay. As sourcers and recruiters, mastering social recruiting becomes an asset to finding, engaging, and hiring the most talented candidates for your organization. Building a strong online presence, establishing networking connections, and promoting job opportunities can significantly enhance your visibility amongst the right candidates.

The future of talent acquisition, in many ways, is aligned with the future of social recruiting. With more people joining social media platforms and sharing their professional lives online, the opportunities for social recruiting will continue to increase. So dive right in, be proactive, and discover the bounty of talents social recruiting has to offer!

International Recruiting

After exploring various innovative techniques of sourcing, it's essential to delve into the world of international recruiting. You see, in our interconnected world today, talent doesn't stay confined within borders. So, recruiting isn't just about discovering talent within your local landscape or national boundaries anymore; it's much more global. And if you're looking to expand your talent pool and source the crème de la crème of professionals, international recruiting is a strategy you can't gloss over.

Let's start by understanding what international recruiting really is. In essence, international recruiting is about finding the right individuals for your organization but from a much larger, global pool of candidates. This tactic allows you not just to broaden your horizon, but it also introduces you to diverse skill sets and multicultural perspectives – crucial elements for innovation and growth in an organization.

International recruiting, though, is not a piece of cake. It's much more than just posting your job on international job boards and hoping the right candidate will stumble upon it. There are different cultural nuances, legal requirements, immigration laws, and even time zones to juggle with. Not to mention, the costs involved in international recruiting are typically higher than local recruiting– travel costs for interviews, relocation packages, and so on.

So, how do we handle this intricate process efficiently? Well, the starting point is building a robust recruitment strategy. It's important to understand the job outlook of different regions, the cultural differences, the popular job boards, salary standards, competition, and legal implications in different countries. Once you have this knowledge, you can tailor your job descriptions, employment offers, and recruiting process to be more appealing for international candidates.

It's also essential to utilize the right tools and platforms to effectively reach out to and engage with international talent. LinkedIn, for instance, is a platform that spans across countries and industries, making it a beneficial resource for international recruiting. Various international job boards, online communities, and professional networks should also be part of your recruiting arsenal.

Now, if you are like most recruiters and the idea of coordinating calls across three different time zones doesn't thrill you, consider leveraging technology to streamline the process. Video interviewing and recruiting software can make the initial screening of international candidates easier and more cost-effective. But technology, though handy, doesn't replace the human touch.

That's where cultural understanding comes into play. A candidate in Japan, for instance, will have different expectations and cultural norms than a candidate in Germany. So, understanding, respecting, and accommodating these differences can dramatically improve your communication and relationship with international candidates, influencing their decision to join your organisation.

On another note, consider the legal aspects linked with international recruiting. Each country has its unique set of employment laws, and breaching them unknowingly could lead to significant legal repercussions for your organization. Immigration laws are another pivotal aspect in international recruiting. Understanding the nuances of work permits and visa requirements, as well as helping your candidates through that process, can dramatically ease the recruiting process.

Of course, all this doesn't mean you should just dive headfirst into international recruiting. It's essential to calculate the costs associated with it too. International recruiting tends to be more expensive than local recruiting due to travel and relocation expenses, higher salary bands, and so on. However, if the skills and experiences brought onboard justify these costs, then international recruiting becomes a worthy investment.

And finally, once you've successfully recruited a candidate, that's when the real challenge begins– keeping them engaged and helping them integrate into your work culture. Providing cultural training, assigning a local mentor, and creating a culturally inclusive work environment is key to retaining the top international talent your hard work fetched.

To sum up, international recruiting may seem like a lot of work, and let's be real– it is. But the payoff, the darting perspectives, the diverse skills sets and the richness of experience that international talent brings to the table makes it worth it. So, go ahead, make your move, recruit from the world, and watch your organization thrive!

Remember, as with any recruiting strategy, it's critical to constantly monitor, evaluate, and fine-tune your technique based on your experiences to keep improving and meeting your talent acquisition goals. So, step back, reflect, refine, and then go ahead, recruit the world!

Chapter 3:
Attract & Engage

Talent acquisition isn't just about discovering the right individuals; it's about persuading them to join your team, making them believe that your organization is the correct fit for their career path. This chapter will explore how to rightly grab and maintain their attention, starting with understanding candidate attraction - digging deeper into the importance of employment branding, the power of advertisements, and the stellar role social media can play. Then, we'll delve into how to engage the candidates most effectively. Here, you'll learn to apply marketing principles to recruiting, harness current technology, and fine-tune your interpersonal communication. We'll talk about what it means to bring a personal touch to recruiting and how it can revolutionize your interaction with potential hires. Remember, the line between an interested candidate and a committed new hire is the art of the attract and engage strategy! So, in this chapter, we're going to give you the tools to master that art, setting you on the path of becoming a highly effective recruiter in the competitive world of talent acquisition.

Understanding Candidate Attraction

Now that you've submerged yourself into the wide pool of talent acquisition strategies, let's delve into the intricacies of understanding candidate attraction. At its core, candidate attraction is about creating a narrative that showcases your organization in its most flattering light.

But, it's more than just a simple siren call for talent, it's a strategic feature in your hiring playbook.

Think about it like being on a first date. You want to make a good impression, right? Just like on a date, the best strategy to attract a candidate starts with being a good listener. You need to understand what your ideal candidates are seeking in an employer. What kind of environment are they seeking? What incentives will lure them? Maybe they're looking for challenging tasks, opportunities to learn, or even flexibility to maintain a good work-life balance. These are just some of the points to consider.

Once you've listened and understood what your candidates are looking for, it's time to show them how your organization can offer that. Here, honesty is key - you're not trying to make false promises or fabricate an image of your company just to attract talent. You're trying to showcase how your company's existing culture and benefits can meet their needs.

The whole process of candidate attraction is nothing short of an art form. It, much like creating a master painting, is about finding that perfect balance. The perfect harmony between what potential employees are looking for and what your company has to offer. When your organization's values and opportunities sync up with a candidate's wants and needs, you've struck gold.

Remember, the objective isn't just to get any candidate, but the right ones. A company can attract hundreds of applicants, but if they aren't the right fit for the roles you have, all you really have is a numbers game that doesn't always translate to the right hires. Candidate attraction isn't about collecting resumes. It's more about gaining the interest of quality candidates who align with your company's goals and culture.

Let's talk about perception for a moment, as it's core to understanding candidate attraction. We live in an age where our online presence holds significant value and this extends to a company's image too. The image you present can make or break your ability to attract candidates. If your online existence is inconsistent, unorganized, or portrays a negative company culture, candidates may very well shy away from your job postings.

How you position your employer brand in the market can drastically color the perception potential candidates have of your organization. An impactive, positive perception not only draws candidates to your organization, but it also ensures that those attracted align with your company's values and vision. Would you willingly walk into a den of negativity? Didn't think so. The same applies here - candidates are far more likely to apply to companies they perceive positively.

Next, there's also the power of accessibility to consider. It's not enough for potential candidates to know that you have open vacancies - they also need an easy route to access these opportunities. The application process needs to be clear and straightforward. Furthermore, how you communicate during the application process plays a crucial role too. Quick response times and transparency help keep candidates engaged and can drastically improve the overall candidate experience.

These attraction strategies, mind you, are never static. Each generation of job seekers brings its own concerns, expectations, and demands, altering the landscape of candidate attraction. It's crucial to stay on top of these shifts. What attracted millennials ten years ago may not work as well with the current generation of fresh-faced candidates. Thus, a successful talent acquisition team constantly evolves its strategies, keeping its finger on the pulse of what the workforce wants.

Another important consideration is the competition. Since potential candidates will most likely also be considering other opportunities, it's important not just to know what you have to offer, but also what your competition offers. After all, knowing the competitive scene and standing out from it can make a world of difference when it comes to candidate attraction.

Finally, candidate attraction is not a one-and-done deal. It's important to revisit, revise, and revitalize your strategies as per the feedback and performance metrics. If a strategy isn't yielding the desired results, take a step back, analyze it, and change things up as needed. It's a continuous process of learning and adapting that yields the best results.

Understanding candidate attraction is a crucial cog in the wheel of talent acquisition. By finding creative ways to illustrate the unique aspects of your company and its culture, you can draw in top talent. Remember, the ebb and flow of the job market are perpetual. Being able to drown out the noise and make your company heard through it all; that's the real art of candidate attraction.

Employment Branding is a gem in the business world. The magic is in its inherent power of bringing talent to the company's doorstep. Imagine being in a position where you don't have to go out hunting for talent, but the talent comes knocking on your door! Feels like daydreaming, right? Well, that's the magnetism of a strong employment brand.

A well-crafted brand paints a vivid picture of what it's like working in your organization. It tells potential employees about the culture, working conditions, benefits, and growth opportunities. Good branding isn't about sugar-coating the reality or creating a facade; it's about depicting the truth in the most appealing way.

Employment branding is not just about attracting potential hires, but it's about attracting the right kind of talent. The brand messaging needs to be in line with the company's values, mission, and strategic direction. Otherwise, you'll end up attracting candidates who may not be an excellent cultural fit, which can lead to poor retention.

Branding is a constant exercise, and it's more about the journey than the destination. It requires consistent efforts and innovative thinking. It's not about just creating a pretty career website or a catchy company slogan. It involves a deep level of engagement with employees and an in-depth understanding of what your company stands for.

Engagement is the key here. It brings life to the brand, and it's about leveraging every opportunity to create positive experiences for potential, current, and past employees. This can be achieved through various platforms such as social media, company blogs, and recruitment ads.

Remember, your employees are your brand ambassadors. They play a crucial role in shaping the perception of your employment brand. Hence, their engagement level directly impacts the brand's strength. Happy and engaged employees would share their positive experiences, which in turn can attract more like-minded individuals.

It's interesting how the branding tactics can be varied based on the target audience. For instance, if you're trying to attract fresh graduates, campus recruitment, internships, and online platforms can be strategically leveraged. Contrastingly, for executive level hiring, the branding strategies need to be more about showcasing leadership opportunities, challenging work, and growth potential.

Now, let's dive into the element of authenticity. As we said, branding is not about creating a facade. It's about staying true to who you are as an organization. This might sound somewhat cliché, but it can't be emphasized enough. Authenticity builds trust and attracts people who genuinely resonate with what you stand for.

However, authenticity doesn't mean unveiling your company's flaws without any consideration. Rather, it means acknowledging the areas of improvement and showcasing efforts taken towards betterment. After all, no company's perfect and candidates understand that too! It's the determination to improve that makes a difference.

To create an effective brand, it's crucial to understand the changing paradigms of the talent market. With the advent of remote work and increasingly diverse workforces, the employment brand must cater to a wider audience. It should be inclusive, appealing and flexible to accommodate different work life models.

Crafting an effective brand is no small feat. However, once you've established your brand effectively and broadened its visibility, the rewards are enormous. When your organization becomes a desired destination for talent, it can dramatically lessen the load on the recruitment process.

Every company has a unique story. As talent acquisition professionals, it's about using it to create an indelible impression on potential candidates. It's about making them feel excited about the prospect of being a part of that story.

Well, that's the nutshell of employment branding. Sounds challenging, yet exciting, right? In the realm of talent acquisition, it's an endless journey of creativity, authenticity and constant engagement. It's about making your organization not just a place to work, but a place to grow, thrive and fulfill dreams.

So, next time you think about talent acquisition, remember the power of building an inviting employment branding. Understand that it's not just a part of your strategy, but it forms the epicenter of your talent acquisition plan. Sprinkle some creativity, weave in your unique story and voila you have got yourself a powerful employment brand.

Ultimately, employment branding is a world where your potential employees get to see what's in for them even before they step into the organization. It's all about weaving an enthralling tale that attracts people, ignites their passion, and inspires them to be part of the journey ahead. That's the power of employment branding, and that's the wave, you, as a talent acquisition professional, should be riding on!

Advertisements are a staple to any talent acquisition regimen. They're an indispensable tool in your recruitment toolbox, and rightly so. When implemented effectively, advertisements not only attract prospective candidates but also help you shape and sell your company's narrative. These are your megaphones, your banners held high, a key part of how you tell your company's story to the world. So let's talk about getting it right.

First things first, a good job advertisement should spell out exactly what the role entails. Yeah, wizard with words are engaging but remember this isn't a shell game. You don't want candidates applying for roles they don't understand or worse, aren't qualified for. So skip the jargon and be clear, precise about the job role. Also, avoid the kitchen sink syndrome. No need to beguile the reader with every single task included - focus on the key requirements and responsibilities.

Now let's get something straight, just like your morning coffee, one size doesn't fit all. Tailor your advertisements to the demographic you're targetting. Recent graduates might value training opportunities while experienced professionals could value the opportunity to lead or innovate. Understand your candidates, their needs and create a message that resonates with them. Remember, to recruit the best talent, your message must be enticing, engaging, and distinctly 'you'.

Behold the power of storytelling - it's how you engage your prospects. Your job advertisement should not just convey the position's duties and requirements but also why they should work for your organization. Be enthusiastic about what your company does, the opportunities it offers, why it's a dynamic great place to work. Let your passion for your company shine through. But here, subtlety is key. You want to avoid sounding boastful or exaggerating, that's outright off-putting!

Tap into the Benefits

Remember, the job advertisement is no place for modesty. Don't shy away from touting your organization's benefits. It's not bragging if it's based on facts. Does your company provide super healthcare benefits or supports flexible working? Does it have a commit to professional growth with programs like mentoring, coaching? Or perhaps it prizes collaboration and employee input? Whatever perks your company offers, make sure they're crystal clear in your job advertisement.

The Importance of Design

First impressions matter, which is why design plays an integral part in your job advertisement. Gritty walls of text can be off-putting, making even the best job opportunity sound dull and monotonous. Plenty of white space, bullet points, sleek design can make your advertisements more engaging. Let's not forget, a visually appealing design speaks volumes about your company's brand and personality. So invest some time, maybe some bucks, in getting your advertisement design right.

Optimize for SEO

It's all well and good crafting sublime, stellar job ad but what good is it if no one sees it. In the digital age, search engine optimization (SEO) is an absolute must. So include relevant keywords and craft compelling meta descriptions. This can help boost your visibility on search engines, job boards, and social media networks, roping in those passive candidates you might otherwise miss. Don't fret! It's simpler than it sounds. Stick to relevancy, precision, and you'll be golden.

Understanding the Platforms

One crucial facet of advertisement strategy is the proper usage of platforms. Different platforms lure different audiences and thus should be used strategically for target demographics. Job boards, for instance, cater to active job seekers, while social platforms like LinkedIn can bring in passive candidates who aren't actively looking. Some might find it intuitive, but you really gotta have a solid grasp on where your potential candidates are already hanging out.

Lastly, advertisements aren't a set and forget kind of deal. Once you have crafted and published your job ad, monitor its performance.

Check application rates, bounce rates, conversions, and make alterations as necessary. Advertisements are part art, part science and require regular tuning to hit their maximum potential. Use your metrics to refine your job ads, learn from every iteration and stir up next-level recruitment results!

So, in a nutshell, treat advertisements as your organization's grand stage to sing its worth. Keep your goal audience in mind and suit your message to resonate with them. Get imaginative,but keep it simple and frank. Remember, each job advertisement is a distinct opportunity to not only fill a role but also enhance your company's reputation and reach! Keep these guidelines in your back pocket and turn your job ads into absolute recruiting powerhouses!

Leveraging Social Media has become an increasingly vital tool within the realm of talent acquisition. The accessibility and reach of various social platforms have made it possible for recruiters to tap into a massive pool of potential candidates. The intention of this section is to provide a comprehensive understanding of how you can effectively harness the power of social media for talent acquisition efforts.

First and foremost, establishing a strong presence on primary social media platforms can increase your chances of sourcing top talent. LinkedIn, Twitter, and Facebook are some of the most-utilized platforms by recruiters. More niche platforms like GitHub, Behance, or even TikTok can also be incredibly valuable depending on the specific roles you're looking to fill.

Why is it so important to establish and maintain a strong social media presence? Simple. It makes you visible and accessible to candidates. But it's more than just making an account and sporadically posting job listings. It's about crafting a distinct online persona that genuinely reflects your brand and culture. Showcasing your core values, current employees, milestones, and behind-the-scenes glimpses can give potential candidates an authentic feel for your company.

Alongside visibility, social media can dramatically widen your pool of potential candidates. Recent studies show an increasing number of job seekers are leveraging social media in their job search - and this trend only looks set to continue. In essence, social media is where the candidates are, and that's where you need to be!

When connecting with potential candidates, remember that it's all about building relationships. Social media provides an ideal platform for initial interaction between recruiters and candidates. When engaging with potential candidates, aim to initiate conversations instead of just sending them a general application form. Personalized messages can make a tremendous difference and cultivate a more meaningful, positive candidate experience.

Next, consider using social media to share compelling, value-driven content that's relevant to your industry. This can range from blog posts, infographics, employee testimonials, webinars, to virtual events. Consistently sharing quality content can position your organization as an industry thought leader, subsequently attracting high-quality candidates.

Furthermore, social media presents an ideal opportunity to leverage employee advocacy. Encouraging your current employees to share job openings, corporate news, and achievements can dramatically increase your reach and visibility. Studies show that job seekers trust the voice of employees more than the company's corporate messages when considering job opportunities.

Now, let's talk about social media advertising for talent acquisition. Targeted ads can help you reach specific demographics, potentially leading you to your next top hire. Plan your strategy carefully, taking into account the demographics of the social platform you're using, along with the kind of candidates you're trying to reach.

Again, keep in mind that each social platform houses its unique audience. It's crucial to know where your target candidates hang out online. Is it more likely to be LinkedIn or Instagram? Use this information to strategize where you'll concentrate your efforts and potentially use targeted ads.

Consider the metrics. As with any other method included in your recruitment strategy, monitor and analyze the success of your strategies on social media. Keep track of likes, shares, comments, click-through-rates, and more. Identifying what's working and recalibrating your approach based on reliable data can prove incredibly beneficial.

Finally, remember that social media is ever-evolving. Adaptability is key. What worked last year may not work today. Always keep an eye out for social media trends and features that can potentially bolster your recruitment efforts.

In conclusion, social media is no longer just a platform for chitchat. It provides vast opportunities for recruiters to source, attract, and engage with potential candidates. However, it requires a thoughtful, personalized, and strategic approach to truly leverage it. If you can master that, the talent acquisition possibilities could be limitless.

Done right, leveraging social media is like throwing your hiring net far and wide – you're sure to haul in some valuable catches. Remember, the more active, interactive, and creative you are, the bigger and better your net becomes. Happy social recruiting!

Engaging the Candidate

The art of talent acquisition doesn't stop at finding the perfect candidate; it's equally important to catch their interest and keep it burning. For this, it's crucial to tailor your strategy according to the individual candidate's needs and expectations rather than a one-size-fits-all approach. After all, we're dealing with people, not products. Knowing what the candidate is passionate about helps to emphasize how the job opportunity aligns with their aspirations. Including personalized conversations in the process increases engagement and creates a sense of connection. It's also key to highlight the unique aspects of the role and the organization and how it can benefit the potential employee. But it's not only about the perks and the paycheck; candidates are increasingly looking for meaningful work and a compatible work culture. Incorporating these elements in your communication effectively piques the candidate's interest while painting a realistic and compelling picture of what working in the organization can offer them.

Applying Marketing Principles in Recruiting. We're at a point now where we're talking more about how to attract and engage potential candidates. It turns out, a lot of what works best comes from good, old-fashioned marketing. Yes, the same marketing strategies used to persuade consumers to buy products can also be effective in persuading prospective candidates to join your team. So let's dig into how to apply marketing principles to recruiting.

First off, let's think about the value of branding. When you're marketing a product or service, one of the first things you develop is a brand identity. This includes a clear message and image that reflect the product's value. The same can be done with jobs and companies. In the context of recruiting, this is often referred to as Employment Branding. By creating a strong and unique employer brand, you'll attract candidates who align with your company's values, culture, and vision.

Next, consider the concept of target marketing. If you're selling a product, there's a particular demographic you're hoping to attract. The same is true for recruiting. You should have a clear understanding of the kind of candidate you want to attract. From there, you can tailor your job postings and recruiting strategies to appeal specifically to that demographic. Like any good marketer, a good recruiter knows their audience.

An understanding of consumer behavior can also prove invaluable in this space. You have to know where your target candidates are, what they're looking for, and how to best deliver your message to them. For instance, LinkedIn might be a prime spot for reaching professionals in corporate roles, while Instagram could be a better platform for capturing the attention of creative associates.

Crafting a compelling message is essential as well. It's not enough to simply list the duties and requirements of a job. In the same way that a good advertisement makes a product seem appealing, a well-crafted job posting should make the role and the company seem attractive to potential candidates. Communicate a sense of excitement and opportunity.

Testimonials and reviews can serve as powerful marketing tools too. As part of a marketing strategy, companies often leverage positive reviews from customers. Similarly, recruiters can use testimonials from current and former employees to enhance their job posts. Such testimonials can add authenticity to the job advert and attract potential candidates who desire similar positive experiences.

Another marketing concept that recruiters can incorporate is the idea of a Call to Action (CTA). In marketing, a CTA is a prompt that encourages a potential customer to take a specific action, such as signing up for a service or purchasing a product. In recruitment, a CTA might encourage a candidate to apply for a job or sign up for job alerts. By providing candidates with clear, action-driven language, you can motivate them to take the first step in the recruitment process.

When it comes to analytics, marketing offers invaluable lessons for recruiters. Campaign tracking and data analysis can provide insight into what's working and what's not, which can inform your recruiting strategy moving forward. This can involve tracking the number of applications received per job post, following the applicant journey, or keeping tabs on the source of hire to determine the most effective channels.

In marketing, we have A/B testing, where you present two versions of the same campaign to separate groups and analyze which one performs better. You can apply the same testing principles in recruitment, by modifying job descriptions or advertisements, for example, to see which iteration attracts more quality applications.

Giving importance to communication and feedback is another principle that applies both in marketing and recruiting. Develop a communication strategy that keeps potential candidates informed and engaged, and be responsive to their inquiries. At the same time, seek their feedback on the recruiting process. This can help you improve your approach and ensure a positive candidate experience.

Also, let's not forget the power of storytelling. A good story can make a product or company more relatable and attractive. Highlighting your company's unique journey, the challenges it's overcome, or what makes your culture stand out, is a great way to engage potential candidates.

Above all, one of the best lessons marketing can teach recruiters is the need for creativity. The marketplace is constantly changing, and recruiters, like their marketing counterparts, must quickly adapt. Creativity is key when it comes to standing out from the crowd and connecting with your target audience in meaningful ways.

Recruiting may not traditionally have been seen as a marketing exercise, but more and more employers are realizing the value of this approach. When you apply marketing principles to your recruiting efforts, you bring a new level of strategy and creativity to your approach. This can help you successfully attract, reach out to, and engage high-quality candidates who could be perfect for your team. As recruitment evolves, the lines between it and marketing continue to blur, making for a fascinating blend of these two worlds.

And remember, while these principles hold true for most, recruiting is also about building relationships. Beyond marketing your company and attracting candidates, it's about creating an environment where people feel valued, recognized, and excited to contribute to the company's success. By incorporating marketing principles into a recruiting strategy built on genuine care for candidates, you're sure to attract the right talent, at the right time, for the right roles.

Incorporating Current Technology can spike up your talent acquisition game. Today's world is marked by technological advancements that impact all spheres of life, recruitment inclusive. The changing narrative means that as a modern-day talent acquisition specialist, your proficiency isn't just on the traditional aspects. Technology fluency forms a fundamental part of your skills toolbox. And there's a lot to love about technology when integrated efficiently into your recruitment tactics.

The exciting world of technology provides an array of tools to transform your recruitment strategies and tactics. Take Applicant Tracking Systems (ATS) for starters. This incredible tool offers a centralized platform to manage job postings, applicant status, and communication. See how it goes? You get to kill multiple birds with a single stone. Or as some would say, a heck of a smart move.

Now, consider the power of analytics and Big Data. Recruitment metrics can be overwhelming with numbers flying everywhere. But get your hands on a good analytics tool? Say hello to simplified data analysis, pinpoint accuracy in future talent predictions, and magically making sense out of the complicated recruitment numbers. It's like having your personal fortune teller, only a bit more reliable (wink!).

Then, there are video interviewing tools. You've got a candidate in a different time zone? No problem. A video call can fix that real quick. Get this, you can record these interviews and share them with your team for collective decision making. This also means excluding those unnecessary multiple interview rounds – all thanks to technology.

Don't overlook the power of AI. You can automate routine tasks, sift through large volumes of CVs in a snap, and even provide instant responses to candidate inquiries. You know what that means, right? More time for you to concentrate on core recruitment tasks. Let's face it, nothing could be handier in an age where time is of the essence.

Now, we're also living in a socially connected world. Social media platforms are a potential goldmine for talent sourcing. LinkedIn, Facebook, Twitter, Instagram, and more offer vast networks to tap into. Post a job, share your company's vision, interact with potential talent - the possibilities are positively endless with social media.

On the flip side, technology doesn't come without its headaches. One issue is the potential data breach threats that could pose severe challenges. Unauthorized access to sensitive data could lead to severe privacy infringements, and that's a territory you don't want to find yourself navigating.

Then, there's the challenge of technology misuse. Without the right knowledge and expertise, technology may just end up being a costly fancy tool in the recruitment toolbox. A key to a powerful car doesn't necessarily make one a great driver. The same applies to technology in talent acquisition. It can only be effective when properly used.

Truth be told, technology wouldn't replace human talent acquisition professionals - well, not entirely at least. Despite the apparent benefits, technology should be viewed as an enabler rather than a replacement. The human touch, such as emotional intelligence in decision making, can't be automated after all.

So, you may ask, how do you incorporate current technology in your talent acquisition process? Well, it begins with understanding your recruitment needs. Understand your workflow and identify areas where technology could do wonders.

Next, familiarize yourself with various technological offerings. Not every tool out there may be necessary for your recruitment process. Handpicking the right tools that suit your needs best would be a decided advantage. Also, continuous learning is vital for staying tech-savvy. So, always be on the lookout for evolving tech trends.

Finally, don't lose sight of the purpose behind the tech – to attract and engage top talent. The technology you adopt should always work to facilitate this end. If not, it might be a good time to reconsider your options.

In conclusion, technology is becoming increasingly integral to talent acquisition. Despite the challenges it presents, we can't ignore its potential. So, whether you're a newbie or an experienced professional, the readiness to incorporate technology in your talent acquisition process is crucial – if not inevitable. Remember, the technological wave is here, so why not surf it?

Professional Interpersonal Communication Communication, particularly the interpersonal type, is fundamental to successful talent acquisition efforts. It's all about how we exchange ideas, messages, and information with one another. Whether in-person, over email, or on a video call, each interaction brings us closer to securing top talent for the company.

Remember that each conversation you hold as a recruiter or talent acquisition specialist is a unique opportunity to express your company's brand and values. So make conscious choices about the words you use, your tone of voice, and your body language. It's important to keep these communications clear, concise, and professional at all times.

Interpersonal communication in the realm of talent acquisition isn't just a one way street. Listening and showing empathy are also crucial skills. When you take the time to sincerely understand a potential candidate's motivations, aspirations, and concerns, it forms a deeper connection that fosters trust and credibility.

Effective communication also means being transparent about what the candidate can realistically expect from the position, the company culture, and the overall career progression path. Even if the news isn't all sunshine and rainbows, honesty builds respect, exhibiting that you value them enough to be truthful about the opportunities and drawbacks the role may present.

What you say can significantly influence a candidate's perception of your organization, but how you say it also matters. Be attentive about spotting non-verbal cues or signals during initial screenings or interviews. These subtle body language signs could offer valuable insights about a person's suitability for the role, beyond what's on their resume.

Given that we live in a diverse and multicultural world, understanding and appreciating cultural communication norms is pivotal in avoiding misunderstandings and fostering inclusivity. Knowing how to communicate effectively with candidates of varied backgrounds can go a long way in promoting diversity within the company.

In the corporate world, it's essential to maintain decorum and civility. However, in their quest to relate to candidates, recruiters are sometimes tempted to overly personalize the conversation or cross professional boundaries. There is a delicate balance between developing a personal rapport and keeping the conversation strictly professional. So, it's vital to master the art of 'professional friendliness' and maintain that balance.

The ability to communicate a company's brand story compellingly can set your firm apart in the eyes of prospective candidates. Therefore, it's essential to be well-versed with the organization's vision, mission, and values, and find engaging ways to communicate these aspects.

Respecting a candidate's time is another aspect of professional interpersonal communication. This includes timely responses to emails, acknowledging their questions or concerns promptly, and providing consistent feedback throughout the recruitment process. When you respect the candidate's time, they inherently reciprocate the same respect for your process and your organization's time.

Moreover, recruiters often communicate with candidates under stressful conditions, such as job interviews or salary negotiations.

Understanding how to manage these touchpoints through effective communication can drastically improve a candidate's overall experience with the organization, regardless of whether they get selected or not.

In the end, the key is to build meaningful relationships. Remember, professional interpersonal communication isn't just about communicating effectively but also about creating value for everyone involved. It's about resonating with the candidate's journey, professional aspirations, and personal values, while simultaneously portraying your organization's brand and mission in a favorable light.

As a recruiting professional, enhancing your interpersonal communication skills is an investment that will undoubtedly pay dividends throughout your career. It can positively impact your relationships with candidates, colleagues, and hiring managers, ultimately stimulating a more efficient, effective, and empathetic recruiting function.

So, to foster successful recruiting efforts, personal growth in the area of professional interpersonal communication is paramount. Enriching your communications will inevitably lead to positive candidate experiences, ultimately helping you attract and secure the talent your organization needs to thrive.

Bringing Personal Touch to Recruiting Technology has revolutionized the world of recruiting, making it easier to find and reach potential candidates. That said, recruiters can't afford to overlook a critical part of human connection and personal touch in their practices. Personal touch matters, and it couldn't be more critical in talent acquisition. It's a way to stand out in a sea of automated emails and mass messaging. Let's take a deep dive into why a personal touch is necessary and how to incorporate it into your recruiting strategies.

First off, what do we mean by a 'personal touch'? It's practicing recruitment with empathy, understanding, and connection. It's the genuine interest in the candidate's needs, desires, fears, and ambitions. It's about getting to know the person behind the resume and understanding their unique situation. A job application isn't just a name and a list of skills, it's a person considering an important change, and that deserves consideration and respect.

Job candidates often feel like they're sending their resumes into a black hole. Automated responses are usually the norm, which can make candidates feel lost and forgotten. Creating a personalized approach, like a tailor-made email or a phone call to discuss their application, can make candidates feel valued and energized about the opportunity.

This leads us to an essential point: recruiters shouldn't be there to solely fill a vacancy; they should be there to build a relationship. Recruiting should be a conversation, not a one-sided affair. When recruiters take the time to listen to the candidates, they learn about their career aspirations, their values, and what motivates them. This information allows recruiters to match them with an organization where they will thrive and contribute significantly.

It's also critical to note that every interaction a candidate has with your organization impacts your employer brand. A positive and personalized recruiting experience can greatly enhance candidates' perceptions of your company, encouraging them to apply again in the future or even refer their colleagues. On the flip side, a cold and impersonal approach can negatively affect your brand's reputation.

Let's talk about how to introduce a personal touch into your recruiting process. One effective method is a simple one: use the candidate's name. Referring to a candidate by their name in emails and conversations shows respect and recognition of their individuality. The difference between a generic 'Dear Applicant' and a 'Dear [Candidate's Name]' is immense.

Next, context is key. Show candidates that you have taken the time to understand their background, skills, and motivators. Tailor your communication to reflect this understanding. This shows the candidates that their application is not just another number in the stack, but is truly valued.

About those impersonal, copy & paste emails for candidate outreach, let's scrap them. Writing personalized emails can be time-consuming, but the effort will pay off. Candidates are more likely to respond to a message that shows an understanding of their profile and career trajectory.

A good follow-up is also a crucial part of a personalized recruitment process. After an interview or meeting, take the time to thank candidates for their time, mention something you discussed, and let them know about the next steps. This lets the candidate know they are more than just a number; they are individuals whose time and effort are valued.

Regardless of the result, giving constructive feedback can go a long way in providing a positive experience for unsuccessful candidates. It shows empathy and understanding and leaves the door open for future opportunities. Even if the candidate wasn't suitable for the role, the detailed feedback increases the chances of them applying for other relevant positions in the future.

Lastly, remember that human connections take time. Building relationships with candidates requires sincere and continued effort. Patience is critical, and quick wins should be carefully balanced with longer-term relationship-building tactics. It's not always about getting candidates on board instantly, but rather creating a robust talent pipeline and nurturing potential candidates for future roles.

There's no shortcut or magic formula for introducing a personal touch in recruiting. It requires thoughtfulness, patience, and empathy. It's a commitment to prioritize human connection in every step of the process, understanding that each candidate is an individual and not just a listing of qualifications on a resume. It's not flashy, but it achieves results.

A recruiter can use the latest technology, innovative search techniques, and strategic plans, but without a personal touch, these efforts can feel cold and impersonal, leaving candidates feeling like just another number. By bringing a personal touch to recruiting, organizations can stand out in the crowded job market, engage with candidates on a deeper level, and ultimately, attract and retain top talent.

In the end, remember that while technology can help streamline the process and make it more efficient, it cannot replace the value of human connection in recruiting. A personal touch in recruiting isn't just a nice-to-have; it's essential in this digital age where authentic human connection often gets lost amid the noise. People are at the heart of any organization, and treating them as such from the start may be your best recruitment strategy yet.

Chapter 4:
Achieve

In the realm of talent acquisition, achievement often revolves around determining how to measure success while constantly striving for improvement. There's a widespread agreement that tracking performance is essential, but despite this, there's not always a clear consensus on the best way to do it. It's true, numbers talk - recruitment rates, time-to-hire statistics, and retention rates are all crucial. Yet, it's also essential to remember that quality counts too. Just filling a vacancy isn't enough; the match needs to be right. And, that's where the real magic lies - in balancing efficiency with precision. Because in our line of work, we're not just making hires, we're shaping the future of companies, and success involves more than just tallying up the totals. So, how does one 'achieve'? How do we consistently hit the mark? Stay tuned, as in this chapter, we'll be delving into performance assessments, the traits of highly effective recruiters, the future landscape of recruiting technology, privacy concerns in our increasingly connected world, and how to keep pushing forward with the wisdom we've gathered along the way.

Overview of Performance Assessment

Having discussed the intricacies of talent acquisition, it's crucial we dive into a key aspect of the process: performance assessment. The crux is, you can't manage what you can't measure. So, keep your pen ready, let's take a deep dive into performance analysis!

Performance assessments help quantitatively gauge the efficacy of recruiters and shed light on potential areas of improvement. A keen sense of evaluation is crucial in gauging both the efficiency and effectiveness of talent acquisition strategies and methodologies. Without an accurate, comprehensive performance assessment in place, it's impossible to effectively manage your talent acquisition unit.

Talking about the assessment tools, they come in various shapes and sizes, catering to different sets of functionalities. These may range from basic recruitment analytics to granular performance tracking, allowing a comprehensive overview of recruiter productivity. Whether it's tracking applications per job opening or measuring response rate, these metrics serve as a yardstick for assessing performance.

Let's talk a bit about candidate quality. A common fallacy is to equate the number of hires made with successful recruiting. If only it were that simple! Quantity doesn't necessarily translate into quality. That's why it's critical that performance assessment includes an evaluation of candidate quality. After all, your goal is to find the right candidate for the job, not just any candidate.

Moreover, an effective performance assessment entails measuring not only the outcome but also the efficiency of the process. It all comes down to return-on-investment. Spot efficiency issues like wastage of resources or time, and you're halfway to improving the recruiting process. Keep an eye out for the bottlenecks in your workflow that might be gumming up the works.

Another angle worth exploring in performance assessment is the candidate experience. In today's competitive environment, the candidate experience matters as much as the candidate quality. Tracking candidate satisfaction can provide useful insights into where you might be losing potential recruits or how to make the hiring process more appealing.

You may be thinking, 'All that sounds dandy, but what metrics should I use?' Well, when it comes to quantifying performance, there's a smorgasbord of key performance indicators (KPIs) available. Time-to-fill, quality of hire, offer acceptance rate, the list goes on. The trick is determining which metrics are crucial for your organization. You have to choose those KPIs that align with your strategic objectives.

This raises a crucial aspect of performance assessment, the consistency of metrics. Once you have chosen your metrics, it's critical to stick to them. Changing metrics frequently can lead to inconsistent data and faulty performance reviews. Consistency ensures that you are making apples-to-apples comparisons over time.

The truth is, even after establishing the correct metrics and keeping them consistent, challenges may arise. Occasionally, recruiters might find themselves doing a lot but achieving little. It's essential to practice continuous monitoring of metrics, to ensure metrics accurately represent recruiter performance. Where they don't, it may be necessary to adjust your metrics to avoid penalizing recruiters unfairly.

The performance assessment process sounds intense, doesn't it? It is! After all, the goal is to maximize the effectiveness and value of your talent acquisition efforts. That being said, don't let the process become a chore - there's nothing stopping you from turning it into an engaging, productive, and rewarding experience.

Lastly, it's worth reminding ourselves that assessment shouldn't merely be a dispassionate calculation. Realize the human aspect of performance assessment, the celebration of achievements, or the acknowledgment of effort. Performance assessment isn't just about numbers; it's about people too.

In essence, performance assessment is a powerful instrument in the toolbox of talent acquisition leaders. It enables them to gauge their team's productivity, take informed decisions, spot bottlenecks, and continuously improve the recruiting process. Remember, a well-implemented performance assessment framework can make a world of difference!

Let's keep this dialogue going. In the next section, we're hitting the road to discuss good habits of effective recruiters. Stay tuned and let's ride the wind of this exciting journey of learning together.

Good Habits of Effective Recruiters

Let's dive right into the heart of talent acquisition - the habits that separate the average recruiters from the great ones. These practices can serve as a valuable guidepost, helping you navigate your career in talent acquisition and become an effective recruiter.

The first and arguably most important habit: effective recruiters understand their industry inside out. They keep themselves updated on industry trends, changes, and players. This not only helps them match a candidate's skills and experience with the right job but also enables them to provide valuable industry insights with both the candidate and the hiring manager. To put things clearly, knowing your industry is more than just being good at your job. It's about being able to add value to every interaction you have within your professional realm.

Furthermore, communication is the lifeblood of effective recruiters. While this might seem like a no-brainer, strong communication skills encompass more than just being able to articulate thoughts and ideas. It involves active listening, empathy, and reflection. An effective recruiter plays multiple roles at the same time - a counselor, coach, negotiator, and salesperson. Each of these roles requires its own unique communication skill set.

The third habit is building strong relationships. Recruitment isn't a one-time transaction. It's an ongoing process of building and maintaining relationships with both candidates and hiring managers. This means staying in touch even after a candidate has been placed. Not only does this keep you on the top of a candidate's mind in case they consider changing jobs in the future, but it also fosters trust and goodwill which can lead to referrals down the line.

Next up is leveraging technology. One of the hallmarks of a good recruiter is the ability to keep pace with technology. In an age where data and technology go hand in hand, understanding how to leverage software, automation, and analytic tools to improve sourcing, engage candidates and track metrics is crucial to staying competitive.

Agility is another crucial trait of an effective recruiter. The realm of talent acquisition is ever-changing, thanks to the competitive nature of today's job market. Because of this, recruiters need to be nimble, flexible, and ready to adjust their strategies as and when needed. Being adaptable also means keeping an open mind to new techniques, tools, and trends.

Then there is the habit of being proactive. A solid recruiting strategy is essential, no doubt. But, exceptional recruiters understand that there's an element of proactiveness involved. They don't wait for the right candidate to stumble upon their job posting. Instead, they actively seek out talent, reach out to potential candidates, and maintain a pipeline of qualified candidates.

Another good habit is commitment to continuous learning. The world of recruiting is fast-paced and ever-changing. Effective recruiters understand that to stay at the forefront of the industry, they need to commit themselves to continuous learning. This can be achieved through regular training, attending webinars, participating in industry events, and reading up on the latest trends in HR and recruiting.

An effective recruiter knows the importance of candidate experience. They endeavor to make the hiring process seamless and engaging for candidates—from the first contact right through to onboarding, ensuring a good impression of the organization even if the candidate doesn't land the job. More than just a courteous practice, the quality of a candidate's experience influences their decision to accept a job offer, reapply in the future, or even recommend the company to others.

One more thing worth noting - good recruiters have a knack for identifying potential. They don't just look at what the candidate can do now but what they could do in the future. This involves looking beyond the resume and getting a feel for a person's attributes - their attitude, eagerness to learn, ability to adapt, emotional intelligence, and more.

Lastly, great recruiters consider ethics and integrity to be non-negotiable. They ensure transparent communication and treat every candidate fairly. A professional recruiter knows that their behavior reflects the company's reputation and works diligently to uphold a high standard of conduct.

In summary, being a great recruiter is no small feat. It involves a multi-faceted approach, combining industry knowledge with soft skills, emotional intelligence, tech-savviness, agility, and above all, integrity. You might consider yourself to be a good recruiter, but striving for these habits can transform you into an exceptional one.

Now that we've explored the habits that distinguish effective recruiters, it's time to translate these learnings into action. Remember, being effective at what you do is a journey rather than a destination. Every interaction, every placement, and every hurdle offers the opportunity to refine these habits and become a better recruiter.

Fear not; the road to becoming an effective recruiter might be filled with challenges, but it's a rewarding journey that promises both personal and professional growth. Embrace the learnings, celebrate the victories, and relish the opportunity to make a real difference in people's lives and your organization. Now, let's forge ahead to explore the future of recruiting technology.

Looking Toward the Future of Recruiting Technology

As we continue our exploration into how we can streamline and improve recruitment through technology, it's essential to gaze further ahead. It's not enough to just stay in the loop or become acquainted with the latest software and tools. To truly achieve excellence in talent acquisition, we must anticipate the future of recruiting technology. So, let's venture into the fascinating developments we can expect to see in the not-too-distant future.

Artificial intelligence (AI) is undoubtedly one of the major drivers of technology across industries, and recruiting is no exception. Employing AI in recruitment seems like a no-brainer. Imagine a system that can sift through mountains of resumes, picking out the perfect candidate profiles in record time. The use of AI can significantly cut down the time taken to shortlist applications and can also accurately match candidates with job profiles.

Not only that, AI-powered chatbots can provide lightning-fast responses to candidate inquiries, keeping potential hires engaged even outside office hours. These chatbots are improving all the time, becoming more conversational and less robotic each passing day. We can expect them to play a much larger role in the near future, managing everything from setting up interviews to answering complex questions about company culture or benefits.

Furthermore, predictive analytics is another impressive tech innovation with a promising future in recruiting. If we think about recruiting as a game of chess, predictive analytics gives us the ability to plan our moves several turns in advance. By analyzing historic data, these analytical tools can identify patterns and trends, making it possible to forecast hiring needs accurately. This could revolutionize workforce planning, preparation, and budget allocations.

Augmented reality (AR) and virtual reality (VR) might currently be perceived as cutting-edge technology predominantly used in gaming, but their functions could transform the recruitment space. These technologies can be used for virtual firm tours, realistic job simulations, or immersive assessments, giving potential hires a real feel of the job and company environment.

A growing trend in recruitment technology is the shift towards people analytics. Rather than just analyzing recruitment metrics, people analytics encompasses the entire employee life cycle. It delves into engagement, performance, productivity, retention, and many more aspects. This holistic approach will promote a more comprehensive understanding of the dynamics within an organization, thereby allowing more informed decisions.

Another key technology that is expected to shape the future of recruiting is blockchain. By creating a decentralized and secure digital ledger, blockchain can help verify a candidate's professional credentials, educational degrees, and work history in an efficient and indisputable way. This could mitigate the risk of fraudulent applications and enhance the credibility of the recruitment process.

Recruitment marketing platforms will continue to evolve, providing recruiters with even better ways to attract top talent. We're talking about sophisticated algorithms that match job ads to the most qualified audience, comprehensive analytics to measure ad performances, and an easy-to-use interface to manage everything. The future will require recruiters to think more like marketers than ever before.

We can also look forward to technology that fosters inclusivity in recruitment. For instance, AI software that can mitigate unconscious bias in the recruitment process by highlighting diverse applicants and promoting fair hiring practices. It's also expected that there will be more technologies developed that cater to individuals with disabilities, making talent acquisition more accessible.

Remote hiring tools, a sector that has already seen rapid growth, will only continue to become more robust, allowing recruiters to effectively find, assess, and hire talent from across the globe. We can anticipate improved video interviewing tools, more effective screening software, and even remote onboarding processes, further breaking down geographical barriers in talent acquisition.

Additionally, technology will push recruitment towards being data-driven. Take 'big data,' for example. It involves analyzing large sets of data to reveal patterns, trends, and insights that can help in strategic decision-making. With big data, recruiters can predict hiring needs, identify potential issues, and measure the success of recruitment strategies. This can prove to be invaluable in the speedy, dynamic world of talent acquisition.

The emergence of more sophisticated employee referral platforms is another exciting prospect. These platforms expected to leverage advanced AI algorithms can identify high-potential matches within an employee's network, prompting them to make a referral. The future of employee referrals looks not only robust but also smarter, more targeted, and efficient.

Lastly, the use of technology in enhancing the candidate experience cannot be overstated. The future will likely see candidates being able to apply for jobs through mobile apps, receive real-time feedback, and get personalized job recommendations. The objective is clear - to make the application process as smooth, friendly, and human as possible.

In conclusion, the future of recruiting technology appears to be promising, innovative, and more than a tad exciting. As talent acquisition evolves, the possibilities that lie within technology continue to expand. To truly embrace these advancements, recruiters should stay curious, keep learning, and never shy away from being pioneers in utilizing new technology. The future is coming. Let's be ready to meet it head-on!

Privacy Issues in the Digital Age

Talent acquisition in the digital age comes with its unique sets of challenges, one of which is navigating the increasingly complex landscape of data privacy. The digital footprint of candidates has vastly increased, allowing recruiters access to unprecedented amounts of personal information. On one hand, this presents an opportunity to source better-suited candidates for specific roles. On the other hand, it raises concerns about privacy and data protection regulations.

The rise of social networking sites, internet search engines, and digital tools has leveled up the recruitment game. These platforms offer a plethora of candidate information, making it easier for recruiters to profile talent before making contact. Yet, it has also blurred the boundaries between professional and personal lives.

Take LinkedIn for instance, almost a playground for recruiters these days. While it's more than useful to view a candidate's professional CV - it's not always appropriate, or indeed legal, to snuffle around in the personal interests and posts they may also share on this platform. It's a fine line and one that recruiters must abide by both ethically and lawfully.

So, how much information can you reasonably gather from a candidate's digital presence without infringing their privacy? It's a little arcane, isn't it? This part alone, my friends, might make you wonder if it's time to hire a legal team. Well, don't worry, you're not alone.

Data protection laws like the General Data Protection Regulation (GDPR) in Europe, or the California Consumer Privacy Act (CCPA) in the US, aim to enhance privacy rights and provide a framework on how personal data should be collected, stored, and used. Knowledge and compliance with such laws are of the essence in today's recruitment landscape.

Data privacy should not be treated as an afterthought, but woven into the fabric of recruiting strategies. It's essential that recruiters ethically manage candidate information. This includes clearly communicating the purpose of data collection and how it'll be used. After all, candidates appreciate the clarity and this can reinforce your organization's credibility and trust.

Another area recruiters need to be cautious about is the use of artificial intelligence (AI) and machine learning in screening and selection processes. While there are definite benefits to these technologies, there is also a risk that they can infrally on a person's rights and privacy, especially if the algorithms are bias-based or discriminatory.

In this regard, it's important to conduct regular audits of your AI recruiting tools to ensure that they are in compliance with privacy laws and regulations. Also, consider being open about your use of AI in your recruiting process. Candidates are more likely to appreciate and trust a transparent recruitment process, which can further enhance your employer brand.

Achieving success in talent acquisition isn't just about finding and hiring the right people. It's about doing it the right way. Being transparent and ethical in our handling of candidate data plays a key role in securing our reputation in the eyes of candidates, and also safeguarding our organizations from legal complexities.

Candidate data can certainly enhance the recruitment process, providing insights and information that can lead to better hiring decisions. But, this treasure trove of data must be handled responsibly and ethically, with explicit consent and a clear purpose.

So as you scout the digital landscape for talent, remember to place privacy at the center of your hunt. Be clear about why and what you're collecting, be honest about how it'll be used, and be respectful of the laws and regulations that exist to protect candidate privacy.

Moving forward, as new technologies continue to transform the world of recruitment, privacy concerns will continue to be a critical consideration. By keeping these issues at the forefront of our practices and strategies, we can uphold our standards, respect our candidate's rights, and remain adept talent acquisition professionals in the digital age.

So, continue with this awareness and knowledge. Embrace the benefits that the digital age brings to recruitment, but remain vigilant on privacy issues. After all, our success in recruitment depends not only on finding the best talent but managing their data with responsibility and respect.

In the next section, we will delve into how to use the knowledge gained throughout this book to enhance and transform your talent acquisition practices. This will bring you one step closer to achieving your recruitment goals in an ethical, respectful, and compliant way.

Moving Forward with Knowledge

The realm of talent acquisition is all about embracing change. From adapting to new methods of sourcing candidates to navigating evolving legal regulations, the industry is anything but stagnant. Therefore, the driving gear in your talent acquisition motor should always be the quest for knowledge.

Looking towards the future of recruiting technology, the landscape is ripe with potential. With artificial intelligence making strides in easing the process of sourcing, screening and even engaging candidates, the future holds endless possibilities. But remember, as tech gadgets continue to evolve, so should your technological savviness. It's not enough to merely survive amidst the digital storm, you need to strive to thrive, to master the tools of the trade, and use them to your advantage.

Consider privacy issues in the digital age, for instance. The advancement of technology, while providing unparalleled ease and speed, has raised certain concerns. One such concern happens to be data privacy. While sourcing and tracking candidates through digital platforms, it is essential to understand and abide by the legislation and regulations that govern data privacy and protection. Ignorance can lead to costly violations that harm your reputation and credibility, so it's crucial to stay educated and informed about these matters.

On one end, it's about understanding the nuts and bolts of running a successful talent acquisition function, and on the other, it's about constantly updating your knowledge bank. If you want to stay ahead of the pack, then getting comfortable in the seat of perpetual learning is non-negotiable. There's always a better way of doing things, a more efficient method, or a game-changing innovation waiting around the corner, and your ability to spot and leverage it makes all the difference.

But let's not construe moving forward with knowledge as a mere accumulation of information. That's just the tip of the iceberg. The core aspect of it involves understanding how to apply this knowledge in real-time situations. Converting knowledge into action is a crucial skill that's often underrated, yet the essence of effective recruiting lies right there.

Enhancing your knowledge also goes beyond staying on top of industry trends or technological advancements. It extends into understanding the intricacies of human behavior, mastering the art of persuasion, and learning how to build authentic relationships. Remember, at its heart, recruiting is a people-centric profession. So, honing your interpersonal skills, empathy, and emotional intelligence is equally significant.

Moreover, education and knowledge do not always come packaged in a conventional form. Sometimes, a simple chat with a colleague, an enlightening podcast, or even a tweet could be the source of an insightful learning or idea. Adopt an open mindset, and who knows, you might discover a nugget of wisdom in the most unexpected place!

To move forward with knowledge, you need to invest in your development continuously. Whether it's reading a new book, signing up for a webinar, attending industry conferences, or even going back to school, it's essential to make learning a priority. This investment doesn't just pay dividends in the form of career growth; it also enhances your overall performance and success in talent acquisition.

Balance your quest for learning with one for best practices. Adapting good habits, be it in the form of a disciplined routine, well-defined processes, or balancing work-life spaces, can significantly impact your efficacy. Learn from your peers, mentors, even competitors, and don't hesitate to incorporate their successful habits into your repertoire.

The knowledge journey doesn't end once you reach a milestone or complete a goal. It's an ever-evolving process— a reflection of your career in talent acquisition. The astronomical pace at which talent acquisition technology and strategy are advancing makes the need for continuous learning even more imperative.

Moving forward with knowledge is pivotal for remaining competitive in the dynamic field of talent acquisition. A recruiter who values knowledge builds his toolkit for success. With updated knowledge, you can drive your talent acquisition strategy into the future efficiently and effectively.

In summary, the true power of knowledge lies not merely in its acquisition, but also in its application, refining, and dissemination. The learning journey is a relentless one, but the reward is a robust, efficient, and future-ready talent acquisition function. In the words of Albert Einstein: "Once you stop learning, you start dying." So, stay curious, stay open, and always—always keep moving forward with knowledge.

Conclusion

So, here we are at the end of our journey, exploring the dynamic world of talent acquisition. We've introduced, defined, discovered and interactively engaged with the core concepts this field encompasses, from understanding roles and workflows, through comprehensive identification techniques, to professional interpersonal communication, all the way to the exciting future of recruiting technology. Although it's an intricate web, every piece plays its part in defining the holistic function of talent acquisition. The evolving nature of this profession offers unlimited opportunities to innovate and adapt; yet, it necessitates a solid foundation, a firm grasp on the basics, and a willingness to learn the ropes. Through this book, we've provided a primer, to not only kick-start your journey into the realm of talent acquisition but to also act as a guide, a mentor as you navigate through. Talent acquisition is not just about finding the right candidate; it's about building relationships, evolving with the digital landscape, and maintaining ethical integrity. So, remember, as you step into this world, you're not just a recruiter or a sourcer—a talent acquisition professional is a strategist, a researcher, a networker, a marketer. And most importantly, you're the first step in building a company's most valuable asset—its people.

Final Thoughts and Reflections

The ever-evolving landscape of talent acquisition can be a challenging arena, but one worth conquering. The journey toward mastering the art of finding, engaging, and acquiring top talent is not just about keeping up with the latest trends or using cutting-edge technology. Instead, it's about understanding the intersectionality of discipline, creativity, empathy, and innovation.

The foundation of effective talent acquisition lies in defining clear objectives and expectations, as we've seen. It involves persistent scrutiny, persistent generation of innovative sourcing strategies, and the will to look beyond the obvious. Just as a miner sifts through soil and rocks to find the hidden gems, so must a talent acquisition professional relentlessly seek out the high-quality candidates lurking beneath the surface of the applicant pool.

Finding the talent, however, is only half the battle. Attracting and engaging these candidates necessitates creativity and authenticity. Employment branding and advertisement strategies should accurately represent your company culture, mission, and values. Candid and consistent communication throughout the recruitment process is essential to keep candidates engaged. The era of one-size-fits-all recruiting has ended; today, you must tailor your approach to each candidate, much like a bespoke suit.

It's easy to get wrapped up in the hustle and bustle of recruiting. The rush to find candidates, the anxiety around engagement, and the competition amongst recruiters can all become overwhelming. However, let's not forget to take a step back from the noise and remind ourselves of the human element in recruiting. It's about listening, empathizing, and finding the best fit for both the company and the candidate. Our ability to empathize, communicate, and connect on a human level can set us apart in the saturated, tech-oriented recruitment landscape.

Performance assessment may seem like an administrative chore, but it's not just about ticking boxes. It's about celebrating achievements, recognizing areas for development, and understanding the impact of your efforts on the larger team or organization. Effective performance assessment leads to improvement, refinement, and sharpening of your recruiting skills.

As we explore innovation in talent acquisition, we need to navigate the maze of digital footprints, privacy regulations, and ethical considerations. The rise of artificial intelligence, machine learning, and big data has revolutionized recruiting, but they've also put greater responsibility on our shoulders. We must treat candidate data with utmost respect and confidentiality, recognizing that privacy is a non-negotiable right, not a privilege.

Recruiting technology is a powerful tool, but it's not a silver bullet. Potential pitfalls and blind spots can accompany the benefits these technologies offer. Staying on top of upgrades, understanding the implications of automation, and knowing how to effectively balance technology with human touch will be essential skills for recruiters in the digital age.

Integrating these facets into your talent acquisition strategies and processes will not happen overnight. It requires persistance and patience. Sometimes you'll stumble, sometimes your strategies will fail— and that's completely okay. Don't be afraid to experiment, take risks, and learn from your failures. After all, failure is just a stepping stone on the path to success.

As we move forward, bear in mind that recruiting is not merely a transaction; it's a connection. Our job as talent acquisition professionals is not just to fulfill a quota, but to build connections, nurture relationships, and power the growth of organisations. We're not just filling vacancies, we're shaping futures – our organization's, the candidate's, and our own.

The future of talent acquisition is exciting, challenging, and unknown. It's shaped by numerous factors, from technological advancements to evolving candidate expectations, to shifts in the overall employment landscape. Despite these uncertainties, one thing is clear: talent acquisition, at its core, remains a profoundly human endeavor. The ability to forge and maintain relationships, to understand and meet individual needs, will always be foundational.

So, keep refining your skills, adapt to changes, harness the power of technology, but don't lose sight of the essence of your role – to connect individuals with opportunities. As recruiters, we have the power to change lives, accelerate organisational success, and shape the world of work. That's a big responsibility, but it's also a tremendous opportunity.

In conclusion, the pursuit of excellence in talent acquisition is not just about finding the best talent but also about being the best we can be in our roles. After all, we could be the reason why someone gets their dream job or why our company lands the perfect candidate. So let's embrace this unique journey with courage, resilience, and determination, knowing that every step we take is an opportunity to change a life and shape the future of our organisations.